THE LIFE AND LOVES OF
THADDEUS STEVENS

MARK S. SINGEL

SUNBURY
P R E S S
Mechanicsburg, PA USA

Published by Sunbury Press, Inc.
Mechanicsburg, Pennsylvania

SUNBURY
P R E S S

www.sunburypress.com

For information about special discounts for bulk purchases, please contact Sunbury Press Orders Dept. at (855) 338-8359 or orders@sunburypress.com.

To request one of our authors for speaking engagements or book signings, please contact Sunbury Press Publicity Dept. at publicity@sunburypress.com.

ISBN: 978-1-62006-226-5 (Trade paperback)

Library of Congress Control Number: 2019952881

FIRST SUNBURY PRESS EDITION: November 2019

Product of the United States of America
0 1 1 2 3 5 8 13 21 34 55

Set in Adobe Garamond
Designed by Crystal Devine
Cover by Terry Kennedy
Edited by Lawrence Knorr

Continue the Enlightenment!

Contents

Acknowledgments ... [v]
A Note from the Author ... [vii]
Introduction ... [1]

PART ONE: LIVING IN THE "MEANTIME"
Chapter One: August 1816 ... [11]
Chapter Two: June 1821 ... [21]
Chapter Three: August 1823 ... [26]
Chapter Four: January 1824 ... [29]
Chapter Five: September 1824 ... [32]

PART TWO: THE PASSION
Chapter Six: December 1824 ... [53]
Chapter Seven: September 1826 ... [59]
Chapter Eight: June 1831 ... [62]
Chapter Nine: December 1837 ... [69]
Chapter Ten: Lydia Hamilton Smith ... [75]
Chapter Eleven: March 1848 ... [79]
Chapter Twelve: October 1850 ... [81]

PART THREE: THE FIRE
Chapter Thirteen: October 1859 ... [85]
Chapter Fourteen: March 1861 ... [103]
Chapter Fifteen: December 1861 ... [132]
Chapter Sixteen: November 1863 ... [135]
Chapter Seventeen: November 1864 ... [148]

PART FOUR: RECONSTRUCTION
Chapter Eighteen: January 1865 ... [153]
Chapter Nineteen: April 1865 ... [156]

Chapter Twenty: February 1866 ... [158]
Chapter Twenty-one: March 1867 ... [161]
Chapter Twenty-two: February 1868 ... [163]
Chapter Twenty-three: March–May 1868 ... [165]

Epilogue ... [171]
Chronology ... [172]
Appendix A: Remarks of H. C. A. Brooks of Peacham on the
    commemoration of the 100th Anniversary of the Academy ... [177]
Appendix B: Stevens on Reconstruction – To the Citizens of
    Lancaster, Sept. 6, 1865 ... [181]
Appendix C: Opening Remarks to the US Senate at the
    Impeachment Trial of Andrew Johnson, April 27, 1868 ... [188]
Bibliography ... [191]
Index ... [195]
About the Author ... [198]

Acknowledgments

In any credible history of Pennsylvania or, for that matter in any account of nineteenth-century America, Thaddeus Stevens makes occasional appearances. He is usually depicted as a skilled orator and a snarling mastermind of politics; contemptuous of anyone who defied or disagreed with him. Historians have noted his role in the build-up to the Civil War, the conflagration itself, and the reconstruction of the country following the carnage.

Long before he took his turn on the national stage, though, Stevens inserted himself into state politics with acumen and a passion second to none.

Still, his role in the critical debates of the day and the backrooms of power has always been understated. This is probably because southern writers heaped their ire on Stevens for his unyielding abolitionist stand. On the northern side, journalists professed to be anti-slavery but could not bring themselves to condone Stevens' interracial relationships. Thus, the man most responsible for the 13th and 14th amendment is relegated to an asterisk in the history books. The man who saved public education for Pennsylvania's children and the nation's children is an afterthought.

Fortunately, there have been several authors who have attempted to give Thaddeus Stevens his due. An early biography that is the starting point for any Stevens scholar is Richard Nelson Current's *Old Thad Stevens, A Story of Ambition*. Current pulls no punches as he shares the strengths and weaknesses of the man. Similarly, Thomas Woodley's tome *The Great Leveler* is thorough and important. I also note the good work done by Ralph Korngold, Fawn Brodie, and Elsie Singmaster, whose research and observations were essential to my understanding of Stevens.

Of these, it was Fawn Brodie who came closest to addressing the Stevens/Lydia Smith love story. While she stops short of saying that Stevens' obsession with slavery was driven by an infatuation with at least two women of color, she at least allows for the possibility.

It was not until 2005 that a gifted writer by the name of Bradley R. Hoch came out and said it: "[Lydia] Smith . . . remained as Stevens' housekeeper in Lancaster and Washington, D.C. until his death in 1868. Over the years she became more than just his employee. Stevens had finally found the love of his life."

More than any historian or analyst I have encountered, Bradley Hoch, a pediatrician by profession, draws a direct line from the idealism of Stevens' youth to the mountains that he moved as an aging Congressman. Hoch presents Stevens as a prophet and a leader whose vision, like that of Moses, was only partially realized. Another interesting aspect of Hoch's work is the attention to Stevens as a lawyer. He presents Stevens' life story against the backdrop of the groundbreaking cases that he took on. This adds to one of the most complete accountings of the life of Thaddeus Stevens available. Hoch served as the President of the Adams County Historical Society, and his book is a great gift to all students of American history.

I am also indebted to two other scholars. Dr. Beverly Wilson Palmer and her Associate Editor, Holly Byers Ochoa, spent years at Pomona College cataloging and annotating *The Select Papers of Thaddeus Stevens*. Without these two volumes of direct research it would be impossible for anybody to write about Stevens with accuracy.

Hoch, Palmer, and others mentioned in the bibliography are clearly better journalists than me. In fact, *The Life and Loves of Thaddeus Stevens* should not be taken as authoritative. I felt the need to present a more human picture of this great man with an eye to the tumult that surrounded him.

Acknowledgments

Finally, I thank my family and friends who have put up with my stories of Thaddeus Stevens for many years. My wife was supportive of this project from the inception—just as she has been for all our journeys together. Colleagues and staff in my public and private endeavors have been patient with me as well.

A final thank you goes to the folks at Sunbury Press for tightening my prose and helping to shape this story into something readable and enjoyable.

A Note from the Author

Clearly, I have taken some liberties when I presume to hear the personal thoughts of Lincoln and some of Stevens' associates. I have tried to be as historically factual as possible but could not resist taking poetic license on occasion. Like the structure of *Updike's Memories of the Ford Administration*, this book alternates between carefully documented history and some storytelling on my part. Just to make sure that the reader sees the difference, anything that is conjecture or suppositions about conversations or personal feelings of the characters is identified in an alternate font.

Introduction

John Updike may have been Pennsylvania's most gifted writer. I had the honor of meeting him and having him sign my copy of *Memories of the Ford Administration* just a few years before he passed away.

One of his lesser-known works, *Memories of the Ford Administration*, is not about Gerald Ford at all. Like his brilliant trilogy on middle-aged angst (*Rabbit, Run; Rabbit is Rich; Rabbit at Rest*) *Memories* is a contemplation of life itself through the eyes of a keen observer. Set in the Gerald Ford interregnum, a college history professor finds a connection between the life and times of Ford and President James Buchanan.

In *Memories of the Ford Administration*, as in all his works, I am swept away by the mastery of his prose. Alf Clayton and the tragic James Buchanan come alive because his writing is as revealing as a photograph and as stunning as an impressionist painting.

All Pennsylvanians should be grateful for this vitalization of James Buchanan of Lancaster, and I was particularly fascinated by the premise that the unhappy encounter with his fiancée, Ann Coleman, may have dramatically changed history. It is fascinating to speculate that our 15th President could have easily ended up counsel to the Coleman Iron Works in Lancaster and lived as contentedly as a legal cow while the Andrew Jacksons, Stephen Douglasses, Henry Clays, and Jefferson Davises dealt more adroitly with the gathering fury of the Civil War.

In my mind, it is indisputable that Buchanan's reticence, as well-intentioned as it was, was a major cause for the ascendancy of Abraham Lincoln and the reactive position of a much tougher line with the South. The issue of slavery, as Updike points out, was declining of its own weight, and the South could have been amenable to an economical resolution of its differences with the North had Senator Jefferson Davis had a more imaginative negotiating partner in the White House. It is horrifyingly possible that the Civil War might have been averted, and the entire face of history changed—but it is mere speculation.

While Updike's Pennsylvania and artistic credentials are secure with me, there is an observation that I would like to make. There is another Pennsylvanian whose career affected history and whose personal story is the stuff of bestsellers. Consider Thaddeus Stevens. The "Old Commoner" best known for creating and commandeering the all-powerful Reconstruction Committee during the post-civil war, post-Lincoln trauma and for introducing the articles of impeachment against Andrew Johnson, had a long, troubled life of public achievements and private heartbreaks.

Beginning with the tantalizing possibility of his descendence from the scalawag French Count Talleyrand, his crippling disability that left him with a pronounced limp and emotional scars that he carried from his youth, and tracing the brilliance of his oratory and political acumen throughout his career, one must be struck by the uncommon talents and magnetic leadership abilities of this "common" man.

My first real interest in Thaddeus Stevens was sparked by Paul Beers, who served as the venerable historian of the Pennsylvania General Assembly. I had just presided over a tumultuous session of the Senate during which the Democrats were pressing for a massive new state initiative on tax reform, and the Republicans were trying every parliamentary maneuver to "run out the clock" to constitutionally mandated sine die adjournment, thereby killing the tax effort. The debate was acrimonious, the gallery was full, and the measure was passed just minutes before the midnight deadline. That legislative drama, said Beers, was surpassed only by the April 1835 session in which Thad Stevens, a young Assemblyman from Gettysburg, single-handedly saved public education.

What? A speech influencing votes on the House floor? A single voice breaking through the nattering babel of legislative proceedings? A lone hero for the Pennsylvania experiment with common schools that, in time, would be replicated by every state in the nation?—It's true.

For years after Stevens' performance, promoters and detractors alike acknowledged the turning point and the high drama that defied popular pressure and secured for all time the basic right of all citizens to an education. His larger reputation was based on his strong, compassionate position regarding slaves. He was actively involved in freeing slaves and, eventually, with the fledgling Republican Party of Lincoln because of his unbending abolitionist position. He was the "scourge of the South" who attracted fierce enemies during his lifetime. His life was usually in danger for his outspoken views, and the pressure wore heavily on him. He could be caustic and vituperative and, even hobbled by old age and sickness, he stood firm in his last battle for constitutional balance between the President and Congress and the unconditional defeat of slavery.

Stevens served in the Congress during Buchanan's presidency. Buchanan's residence was within Stevens' district, and the Old Commoner made no secret of his bemusement. He was far superior to his constituent-president in intellect and a grasp of the political arts and, no doubt, annoyed at the disparity in the level of prominence that each had attained.

Like Buchanan, Stevens never married. Unlike Buchanan, it was not a matter of unconsummated love. It was worse. It was faithful, abject devotion to one or two who shaped his unyielding commitment to the oppressed and the poor. According to most frank historians who only now will bring themselves to admit it, Stevens was involved with a former slave. Lydia Smith, the beautiful mulatto who cared for Stevens and hid from society for the 25 years of their relationship, was the source of his passion and his frustration.

The racism of whispers that dogged his entire political life manifests itself today by denying Thaddeus Stevens his proper, pivotal role in Pennsylvania and national history. The story that emerges when the pieces are put together culminates in Stevens' last defiant statement: insistence on burial in a modest, non-segregated plot.

The lessons to be learned by today's students and leaders through Stevens' fiery passions and his unfailing willingness to take arms against a sea of troubles are classic. But there is an odd and troubling twist to the story of Thaddeus Stevens. In addition to the numerous titles and descriptions that have been heaped upon Stevens by friend and foe and by legions of historians and a handful of biographers, there is one that may also apply: murderer. A mystery that dates to September 23, 1824 must be unraveled before it is completely clear whether Stevens' restless, sarcastic, unyielding power during the era of the Civil War conflagration was the result of a lifelong penance for a brutal deed done in his young manhood or whether there was an equally crushing sense of loss and pain that drove him.

Biographers have approached Stevens in different ways. Elsie Singmaster wrote a glowing tribute to the man who rose above personal adversity and served as the mast in the storm of racism and slavery. Korngold was more dispassionate and thorough but still skirted the issue of Stevens' early years in Gettysburg and his motivations. Woodley and McCall pored over the papers and documents of the era and came to the same conclusion: there was no conclusion possible. Was Stevens a visionary leader or a curmudgeon haunted by his past—or both?

Richard Nelson Current noted that "millions of Southerners . . . thought Damn Thad Stevens was his name just as they thought damn yankee one word . . . he seemed an agent of the devil out of hell." But even Current who wrote a brilliant and comprehensive account of Stevens in 1942 had only this to say about the "incident": "One story connected the name of the crippled bachelor (Stevens) with the death of a colored girl whose body, *enceinte*, had been found in a roadside ditch."

Thaddeus Stevens makes it into the footnotes of every American history book. He was the driving force, the "dictator of Congress," the unflinching abolitionist and irritant to Presidents who, more than any political figure of the day—except for Abraham Lincoln—changed the direction of the union. Yet, he has been consistently vilified by Southern editors and ignored by academics and the posterity that he did so much to ensure. It is not just a matter of lingering factional differences. To be sure, the South will never forget Stevens' pivotal role in the conflagration. But the lingering doubt about the soul of Thaddeus Stevens causes much pause.

In an interesting exchange of letters between Dr. Robert Fortenbaugh of Gettysburg College and biographer Fawn Brodie, Ms. Brodie recognizes the conundrum:

> The more I pondered, the more I realized the truth of your remark that "no one can write about Thaddeus Stevens unless he knows the Gettysburg story." I have always felt that his was a tragic life, but the Gettysburg incident—however, it may really have happened—serves to deepen the tragedy immeasurably . . . If the (murder) charge was true, then certainly in the remainder of his life, in his forty-year battle for the rights of colored people, Stevens did a long penance. If the girl's death was truly an accident, but Stevens was the possible father of the child, then the idea of a life-long penance may still be a pertinent one. But if he was unjustly accused, then the story of this part of his life must be written differently.

Brodie chronicles a "pathological intensity" that Stevens brought to his life's work but never did quite solve the mystery of Dinah. There is a reason for the confusion. While Stevens was a constant feature of the newspapers of the day, and while he wrote extensively to all the major players in his various roles throughout the turbulence of the mid-1800s, and while there is the usual archive of constituent mail from his state and federal legislative days, there is little else. Personal papers, records, and revealing correspondence from and to Stevens have been destroyed—reportedly by Stevens himself. It is necessary to piece together the truth from fragments and circumstantial evidence surrounding his life.

Murderer or grieving lover? Guilt-ridden crusader or brooding, vindictive inquisitor? Two clues from Stevens' life: the source of his strength in his later years was an attractive younger woman who served as a housekeeper, companion, and more. She, like Dinah, was a mulatto whom Stevens afforded unusual social status for the times despite constant private and public derision and the raised eyebrows of colleagues and editors. Southern papers were brutal, but even the northern editors passed judgment:

> Nobody doubts that Thaddeus Stevens has always been in favor of negro equality, and here, where his domestic arrangements are so well known, his practical recognition of his pet theory is perfectly well understood . . . A personage, not of his race, a female of dusky hue, daily walks the streets of Lancaster when Mr. Stevens is at home. She has presided over the house for years. Even by his own party friends, she is constantly spoken of as Mrs. Stevens, though we fancy that no rite of Mother Church ever gave her a right to it. (*Lancaster Intelligencer*, July 6, 1860)

That he would consort with this other "not of his race" indicates a fearless continuation of the memory of Dinah. Hardly the behavior of a public figure seeking to hide an early incident or the actions of a man seeking to bury a memory.

The second intimation comes from Stevens' own words:

> When you have passed through the romantic period of your existence, and found your warm sympathies and ardent hopes all chilled or blasted; and the milk of human kindness which flows in your breast is in danger of being curdled by the cold ingratitude of those upon whom you have continually bestowed nothing but benefactions, you will learn to appreciate the truth of the remark "that he is a happy man who has one true friend; but he is more truly happy who never has need of a friend." (Stevens papers, vol. 16 as noted in Current, p. 120)

These are not the words of a stinging viper. These are the words of one stung, perhaps, by unrequited love.

I have been looking for a way to express my frustrations with today's political circus. Thoreau said he had been "simmering, simmering" before Emerson's writing "brought [him] to a boil." Similarly, Updike has given me the formula for presenting both my take on Thaddeus Stevens and his relevance to the modern political arena. But mostly, this book is about passion. It is about the kind of love and hate that grips us by the throat and influences our behavior. The vapidity of today treats love and passion as a commodity to be displayed as entertainment on soaps, in movies, on recordings. We are voyeurs settling for peeping in on celebrated passions of the day while we pass up the opportunity to plunge into those bright and dark recesses ourselves so that our passions can take us to depths and heights on the full range of life's adventure.

Carl Jung wrote: "A man who has not passed through the inferno of his passions has never overcome them." In the mid-1800s, orators declaimed with great passion on both sides of the slavery question. Families experienced the sweet pain of a wrenching war that tested the human limits of love and hate. And some, despite their infernos—perhaps because of them—rose to greatness and moved the world.

It was Gabriel Garcia Marquez who unlocked the secret of shaking free of the world's grayness. In the tour-de-force *Love in the Time of Cholera,* the young Fermina Daza is told directly: "Tell him yes even if you are dying of fear, even if you are sorry later because whatever you do, you will be sorry all the rest of your life if you say no."

This book offers an opportunity to view one who said "yes" and towers above the political leaders of today in both his accomplishments and his adherence to his principles. That he was motivated by fierce passions of both love and hate is even more reason to place Thaddeus Stevens in his rightful place of prominence—a summit to which students and leaders can climb, a standard for an age that needs one desperately.

—Mark S. Singel

PART ONE

Living in the "Meantime"

CHAPTER ONE

August 1816

His lame leg tired faster than other parts and already hung limply in the stirrup. The tails of his long black coat hung like a blanket over Cid's hindquarters. Thaddeus Stevens sat erect, attuned to the scenery rushing by. He had not seen another rider along the trail since he crossed into Pennsylvania just north of Bel Air. He preferred it that way.

An accomplished horseman, Thaddeus Stevens held the reins loosely as the horse cantered through the late morning. Spring was painting hints of green on the branches of the fruit trees that lined the path. It was bright and warm, and a variety of bird songs coaxed a grin across the usually grim visage of the new lawyer.

Stevens thought of his introduction to the law profession. He thought of the officious Judge Bland and the loutish Judge Hollingsworth and of the obligatory game of Fip-Loo that, predictably, cleaned him out of the money he had carried for the journey. Strange game, Fip-Loo, with no possible way to beat the odds or the dealer. Stevens wondered how many other neophytes paid their tribute to the barristers of Bel Air.

It was worth it, he thought. There would be nothing wrong with a little socializing within his new fraternity—even if it were a rigged card game.

He managed a broader grin when he thought about the wine. It was General Winder who made it clear that Madeira was the proper lubricant for the bar examination machinery. The committee had consumed two bottles before the questioning began. Mr. Chase was the one who posed the questions as Mr. Stevenson, Mr. Archer, and the judges listened. Judge Hollingsworth raised his bushy white eyebrows then squinted like a hoot owl at the young man standing before the table. "What is the difference between a contingent remainder and an executory devise?"

Stevens' answer: "An executory devise of lands is such a disposition of them by will that thereby no estate vests at the death of the devisor, but only on some future contingency. It differs from a remainder in these very material points: First, it needs no particular estate to support it. Second, that by it a fee-simple, or other less estate, may be limited after a fee-simple. Third, that by this means, a remainder may be limited of a chattel interest, after a particular estate for life created in the same." (Singmaster, 1947, p. 33).

Stevens was an exceptional candidate. His preparation was more than the experience of his clerkship with Judge John Mattock. It was more than the result of his voracious appetite for legal tomes and classic literature. His was an early life of unrelenting challenge and heartbreak that made him wise and cynical beyond his 24 years.

"Simple," thought Stevens, "What's next?"

There were no further questions. Whether the panel had been impressed by the comprehensive understanding demonstrated by this lame young lawyer of such an obscure point of property law or whether the unusual glint in his eyes told them about his determination, the older men croaked among themselves like toads and nodded to each other.

"Cards?" said one. Another harrumphed in the direction of the inn's liquor supply, and Stevens went for two more bottles of Madeira.

From his earliest days in Danville, Vermont, Stevens had dreamed of this day. He wanted to share the news with his mother, who had sacrificed so much and had so little joy in her life. He would write as soon as he reached Lancaster.

He reached up to the neck of his shirt to undo the thin black ribbon wrapped around the stiff collar. A cool gust caught it, and Stevens threw his tie and caution to the wind. He dug his heels into his horse, Cid, and enjoyed his galloping vindication. Rocks and rills raced by as his thoughts raced along with them.

The steely determination that was a hallmark of his later political life was formed in the constant struggle against his poverty and his deformity. He did not make friends easily and took no charity from any quarter. He absorbed the tough lessons of life early and brought two profound characteristics to his life's work: he was completely self-reliant and more immune than most to criticism, and he was fiercely committed to the disadvantaged and oppressed.

It did not surprise him in the slightest that his contemporaries banded together in the York, Pennsylvania area to deny him admission to the bar or that he was required to furnish wine to the bar examination committee before establishing his practice in Lancaster or that he was received with hostility when he began that practice. Stevens would work his way to respectability. ✾

———

As his fame spread and as he assumed an ever-larger prominence on the state and national scene, his detractors spun tales of intrigue and scandal. One story that would repeatedly surface in his political life had Stevens in an intimate relationship with at least one of his mulatto housekeepers. This rumor sprang from his public appearances with Keziah and Dinah, and, of course, the lovely Lydia. His lifelong bachelorhood and his passionate embracing of the anti-slavery would cause editors and opponents, townsfolk, and relatives to cluck tongues throughout his life.

Another fascinating suggestion was that the peoples' advocate, the great commoner, was descended of nobility—of a sort. Gossip had it that Sarah Stevens had a passionate affair with the French Count Talleyrand DePerigord in 1791 or 1792 on one of his several missions to New England. This, said some, accounted for the demise and eventual departure of Joshua Stevens, Thaddeus's father, the shoemaker and drunken town arm wrestler. And it was undeniable: from his earliest days, Thaddeus Stevens was strong, imperturbable, sometimes caustic, always in control. He exhibited the demeanor of a rascal count more than a wretched sot.

Rumors and events would rock and shape Thaddeus Stevens. He would sharpen his political instincts and restless, hard-driving nature to build his reputation in the private and public arenas.

The young lawyer would engender such passions that he would be described later in life as a "vindictive, malignant Caliban."(Brodie, p. 10). A Southern editor by the name of George Drake, who would encounter the stony resolve of Thaddeus Stevens a half-century later would write: ". . . this malicious, pitiless, pauseless enemy of an entire nation—this misanthrope, whose curses of mankind shall be written upon his loathed tomb an awful epitaph—this viperous, heartless, adulterous beast, whose horrid life has converted an 'image of God' in plagiarism of devils . . ." (Brodie, 1959, p. 18)

Samuel Bowles, editor of the Springfield, Massachusetts *Daily Republican,* would write on Thaddeus Stevens' death:" . . . his mark will remain on our Constitution and policy longer than that of Webster, of Clay, or even of Calhoun, the three traditional demigods of the Washington Olympus." (Korngold, 1955)

It was the Pennsylvania countryside; not history, that was spread out before Stevens on this day. And it was the darker nature of his ruminations that occupied his thoughts then.

His father spoke in grunts when he spoke at all. Joshua Stevens was as rugged as the Vermont winters that the family braved. Maybe he and Sarah were closer before the children when the marriage was young and unfettered by what Joshua considered a double curse of two sons born with impairments. That Joshua, Jr. and Thaddeus both had been born with withered limbs meant to their father that they would be of little value in his boot-making shop or the thousand assorted chores required for survival in their crude existence. Furthermore, it was a pointed message, in his Baptist thinking, that not one but two sons should be marked with this divine disfavor.

Or was it more visceral? The bootmaker would have heard the rumors. He remained sober enough to be aware of Charles Maurice Talleyrand de Perigord—French diplomat, statesman, and rogue.

The flaws known of this bon vivant were his affection for American women and his club foot. It was also known that he visited Vermont though it is unclear when and whether he and Sarah Stevens met. The leg deformity of his two eldest sons was enough evidence for Joshua.

Sarah, on the other hand, was kind. Her affection for her boys grew in proportion to Joshua's neglect. Besides, she thought, there was real hope for Thaddy—he of the bright eyes and quick mind. Unlike his older brother, he was deformed only in the left leg, and, with exercise and sheer will, he could function normally, defiantly refusing to acknowledge his lameness.

Thad, she thought, would get proper schooling even if she had to move to Peacham where the academy was located, even if she had to work her fingers to the bone. Her dedication overflowed the tiny log dwelling and spilled over into the community where her nursing skills were in constant demand. She was strong and pretty, and Thad was aware early of the contrast between her and the whiskered, whiskeyed gruffness of his father.

Joshua Stevens left Sarah and reportedly died in the War of 1812. It was Sarah who cooked and washed and tutored and sacrificed for the now four boys. It was Sarah who watched as Thad dragged his leg alongside the snowdrifts scraping it raw on those winter walks to school. For most boys, it was a daily chore; for Thaddeus, it was a challenge for survival.

There was indeed something special about Thaddeus Stevens. His older brother Joshua was debilitated physically, and his two younger brothers, Abner and Allanson, were no match for his intellect. Thaddeus, responding to special care from Sarah, drove himself mercilessly. He stunned his mother and neighbors with his reading and photographic memorization skills. He became an expert rider and swimmer and lifted weights so that his upper body, at least, would be an excellent specimen.

Adversity, which had driven his father to drunken despair, forged in Thaddeus a steely determination that was to serve him well.

———

Cid was galloping furiously now, and Thaddeus imagined himself back in Danville with his beloved mother in 1805. A north wind sliced through the peaks just outside of town and moaned and whistled relentlessly in the darkness. Even on moonlit nights, there was little serenity in Danville. The silver light of the Vermont full moon only illuminated the snow that drifted up like angry grizzlies against the whip of the wind. The snow piled high against the doors of the wooden cabins along his street, and the night air beat an incessant threat on the window latches.

Townsfolk didn't go outdoors in winter; they clustered around fireplaces or pot-bellied stoves. The night was an ordeal, a raging animal that would be somewhat calmer if families could make it to sunrise. Thaddeus Stevens would read his Latin close to the fire. His mother and brothers would have been sleeping for hours, and he was finally beginning to drift in and out of his conjugations and declensions. He had gotten used to the constant ringing of air through crevices in the imperfect jambs and sills in their log home. The rattling and creaking took on a rhythm that was almost soothing. But venture anywhere away from the fire, and the icy fingers of the Vermont winter felt like death.

He put two more logs on the iron grate and hoped that he would awake to more than just embers. He moved to the right side of the room, where all three boys slept in narrow cots. His mother, Sarah, sleeping alone in the house's tiny bedroom attached to the kitchen area, stirred and drew the blankets up past her chin to her nose. Her breath helped warm the bedclothes enough for her to sleep.

An insistent knock on the door awoke Sarah. She was already on her way out the door with lantern and carpetbag in hand when Thaddeus saw her and a neighbor lady who was weeping hysterically. Something about her infant and the spotted fever. Somehow it was Sarah who was needed to save the young life. Without hesitation,

Thaddeus was up and dressed and soon whipping the startled horses as they bounced the rickety family cart from house to house. He would spend the rest of the night and morning watching his mother cradle infants in her hands, applying anodynes, comforting children and parents. It was too late for some, and Thaddeus watched the weakest ones arch their backs and die.

They returned home silently, and when Sarah finally spoke, it was to quote a passage from Euripides that the 13-year-old boy had heard from her before: "Love is all we have, the only way that each can help the other."

He was determined to live. Somehow, he knew he owed it to this saintly woman.

Thaddeus Stevens entered the Peacham Academy in 1809 at the age of 16. Sarah and the other boys had made a collective sacrifice and relocated the entire family so that Thad would have the opportunity for quality education. He was poorer than his classmates, and his lameness brought derision of the cruel, adolescent variety. Thaddeus felt his obligation to succeed was a pact he had with his brothers and his mother, who had extended themselves for him. He was prepared to brave long, wintry walks to the school, suffer the taunts of his peers, and work harder and longer than anybody he knew to fulfill his obligation.

It was at Peacham that he first excelled. His scholarship brought him to the attention of Judge Mattocks, who guided and sponsored his further academic career at Dartmouth. It was also at Peacham that one incident left yet another indelible mark. Thaddeus and eleven other students were involved in the performance of a play—a tragedy that, according to school rules, was to be enacted during the day for the review of the Board of Regents. The group chose instead to proceed with the production at night. Whether this was a theatrical decision or a statement of opposition to school policy, the students found themselves facing a tribunal that made the following pronouncement and demanded written satisfaction from the boys:

. . . the Conduct of Moses Hall, Ephraim Elkins, Thaddeus Stevens, Samuel Merrill, Peter H. Shaw, Isaac Parker, Wilbur Fisk, David Gould, Thomas Weston, Hezekiah R. Cushing, Lyman Martin, Abel Walker and Abiel Hall, Pupils in the Academy, in refusing on the day of public exhibition, being the 4th day of September last, to proceed in their Exhibition in the daytime while the Board were waiting to see their performance, was conduct highly reprehensible. And that their proceeding the exhibit a tragedy in the evening of said Day contrary to the known rules and Orders of the school and the express prohibition of the preceptor were a gross violation of the rules and bylaws of the institution, tending to subvert all order and subordination in said school and to disturb the peace of society, and that they be required to subscribe the following Submission, viz: We, the Subscribers, Students in the Academy at Peacham, having been concerned in the Exhibition of a Tragedy on the evening of the 4th of September, 1811, contrary to the known rules of the Board of Trustees On reflection are convinced that we have done wrong in not paying a suitable respect to the authority of the board and hereby promise that as long as we continue students at this Academy we will observe such rules as the Board may prescribe.

Thaddeus Stevens signed the document, but he was anything but sanguine. In an address delivered by H. A. C. Brooks of Peacham on the commemoration of the 100th anniversary of the Academy, Brooks noted the stubbornness of young Thaddeus Stevens and postulated about the effect that it had on his development: "Thaddeus Stevens . . . yielded only because he could do nothing else; but it was probably the last time his imperial will ever bowed to the will of man."

Brooks saw the school tragedy incident as a metaphor for Stevens' entire life. That this and other occurrences sharpened the resolve of Thaddeus Stevens into a razor-like instrument that he used like a surgeon is undeniable.

The injustice of authority and the taunts of his classmates rang in his ears and would extend to his early days in Gettysburg.

When he was struggling in a one-room law office, colleagues would send poorer accounts to that "lame lawyer on the square." Confident of his abilities and resolve, Thaddeus Stevens would fight oppression whenever he confronted it; he would rage against the beast when it was directed at him. He was determined to prosper and to be heard.

A hundred years after his death, one historian recorded this summary of the life of Thaddeus Stevens:

> STEVENS, THADDEUS (1792–1868), lawyer and politician. As a Pennsylvania congressman (1849–53, 1859–68), Stevens vigorously opposed slavery and led RADICAL REPUBLICANS in forming a RECONSTRUCTION plan for stern treatment of the South. He insisted on strict requirements for readmission of southern states into the Union and was instrumental in denying them seats in Congress. Stevens helped secure passage of the Fourteenth Amendment guaranteeing civil rights and chaired the committee that recommended the impeachment of President Andrew Johnson. (Yanak, 1993, p. 368)

That's all. That is the sound bite on Stevens.

Stevens' legacy would be more profound and more underrepresented than any other figure in American history. He was the driving force behind the taxes needed to prosecute the Civil War and every major issue of the day—tariffs, greenbacks, the Freedman's Bureau, the first major Civil Rights Bill, the 13th, 14th, and 15th Constitutional Amendments and the impeachment proceedings against Andrew Johnson would all bear Stevens clear and indelible stamp. He could be identified in both the capitalization and the tempering of America's "manifest destiny" and the drive to provide pioneers "forty acres and a mule." He would proclaim late in life that his greatest achievement was securing public education as a model for the nation during his time in the Pennsylvania General Assembly.

Not one of his achievements came easily. Nor did he receive credit without constant denigration. He would bring much of the skepticism on himself because he approached his mission with passion. An extreme, reckless passion that saw fits of both love and hate and which was too hot a fire for journalists and historians by which to warm themselves.

It was a similar abandon that was hurtling him toward Lancaster and the life that was looming before him like the great Susquehanna Valley. He had been rejected by the pompous barristers of York, Pennsylvania, even though he was well thought of as a teacher in his first assignment after graduating from Dartmouth College. He aimed his horse and his new life toward a new town and planned to make his mark in Lancaster. This would prove to be short-lived as he found that town to be inhospitable as well. Instead, he would set up shop in Gettysburg—at least for the first phase of his professional life. His departure from Gettysburg would be defiant. He would leave to reconstruct his personal and political life and settle finally in Lancaster much to the chagrin of the bluebloods there. He would serve in the Congressional seat that was home to the 15th President of the United States, and Stevens would take great pleasure in deriding his neighbor and constituent.

Cid was charging down a steep slope toward a creek as Stevens stood up in his stirrups. The horse was plunging toward the remnants of a bridge that could not possibly bear their weight. It was much too late to pull up. Stevens reacted instantaneously to his predicament and leaned low on the horse's neck as he dug his heels furiously into his sides. The horse leaped boldly even as his front hoofs dangled over the chasm. Horse and rider landed in an explosion of dust and limbs just a few feet on the other side. Thaddeus Stevens picked himself up off the ground and walked to the edge of the ravine, where only a few boards from the bridge remained.

At that moment, he heard a whisper that sounded very much like his mother's voice.

"Destiny" was the word that echoed through the cavern and in his head. &

CHAPTER TWO

June 1821

Young Thaddeus Stevens settled into the only piece of furniture in the one-room law office he had rented from James Gettys. It was a wooden chair with a writing table attached and a rack on the lower left for books to be stored close at hand. He had spent only a few days in the large community of Lancaster and found it intolerable. Already a major center of commerce and society, Lancaster was stuffy: it was clear that his fledgling career would have to have more modest surroundings for its beginnings.

Gettys had been kind and forbearing as Stevens fell several months behind in rent. Into the winter months, he would often sit alone reading under heavy blankets to avoid the expense of firewood. ❋

Aside from the occasional charity case or the cast-offs from more established lawyers, he spent much time reading. Alexander Pope's "An Essay on Man" was one of his favorites, and he was attuned to the troubling debate on slavery that was beginning to appear in essays in journals of the day. He had taught at the Academy in York when he first arrived in Pennsylvania in 1815, but he was determined to succeed in law, and

Gettysburg was, he thought, just the place to start. His diligence, even in minor cases, won him grudging respect among his peers.

In early 1817, he appeared before the county judge with a client charged with murder. The man had clubbed another man to death in a jealous rage. Stevens prepared carefully for the case and offered an eloquent and unusual defense: "the defendant was insane." The legal community took note of this approach as it was the first time the insanity defense had ever been recorded. Stevens lost the case, and his client was hanged. Later, Stevens would say that he tried 50 murder cases, and only one was hanged. It was this very first defendant, according to Stevens, who actually was insane.

Stevens' skill and creativity were rewarded with a growing client list.

Judge George W. Woodward, a contemporary and colleague in the U.S. House of Representatives, was no ally of Stevens. Yet in his eulogy, he praised Stevens' skills as a lawyer and a politician:

"He always came with a keen discernment of the strong points of his case, and he spoke to them directly, concisely, and with good effect. His humor was irrepressible and trenchant; sometimes, it cut like a Damascus blade." (Hensel, n.d., p. 12)

As a defense attorney, Stevens used his skills to great advantage. In one murder case, the principal witness for the Commonwealth swore that the accused exclaimed: "By God, I have shot him." Stevens succeeded in getting the witness to acknowledge that the words might have been: "My God, I have shot him." This raised the question for the jury as to whether the accused was proclaiming his deed or exclaiming surprise. Stevens' client was acquitted. (Hensel, n.d., p. 31).

There were countless other legendary displays of Stevens' prowess in the courtroom. His practice became lucrative, and he sought out the high-profile controversies of the day. He was at his best when his moral code matched his professional assignment. This was always the case when he opposed slavery and defended fugitive slaves.

In the summer of 1821, Pennsylvania, like most states, was absorbing the implications of the Missouri Compromise of 1820. Maryland, to the immediate south, had already indicated its insistence on remaining a slave state and supported the notion of allowing new slave states selectively. Pennsylvania, through its leaders, was more aligned with the northeast states, although there was friction along the Mason-Dixon line between businessmen, politicians, and even families.

———

Thad Stevens, at 29, had ceased to be "that lame lawyer on the square" in Gettysburg. Slim and strong with a black mane of hair and piercing blue eyes, Stevens held a jury with his sincerity as effectively as he turned on opposing counsel with his restless power. Indeed, town fathers were urging the young talent to consider running for the town council in the coming year. Slavery was a topic for discussion at barristers' card games, and it was clear that the monied class—his potential political support—was comfortable with the Missouri accommodation.

Stevens found the question at least unsettling but was comfortable with accepting a new client.

Norman Bruce visited the small law office and found Thaddeus Stevens, as usual, alone. He waited while Stevens marked his place in the book he was reading and introduced himself. He was a farmer from Maryland who was in search of a fugitive slave by the name of Charity Butler. The slave girl had accumulated six months' worth of days visiting relatives in Pennsylvania and under the terms of the Fugitive Slave Law refused to return to her master in Maryland. But the law, thought Stevens, was clear: the accumulation was periodic and incidental, and he knew that he could win the case for Bruce.

Charity Butler was small and stern. She withstood the scrutiny of the all-white jury and the judgment of a law that rendered her no better than chattel with a dignity that impressed all. Stevens won the case and smashed Charity Butler's hopes for freedom.

"Pieces of silver," he thought when he received his fee. It was the last time he would defend oppressive laws or slavery in any form. It was the beginning of a lifetime dedicated to abolition and equality. ✻

———

Thaddeus Stevens spoke out against slavery in a public speech in 1823. That a learned lawyer—someone outside the growing protest of the literary crowd—would take arms against slavery was notable. That it was a young politico whose career could be damaged with such defiance was an indication of things to come—and the lingering debt that he owed Charity Butler.

Stevens did run for and win a seat on the town council. In 1824 he was up for reelection and spent the year in the company of a housekeeper named Dinah. Like Charity, Dinah was quick and resourceful. She had a pleasant demeanor that was genuine and trustful—not the feigned obeisance of practiced, older slaves. Dinah's lot had improved with Stevens. She had been freed to work for meager wages in the young lawyer's household. She was one of many who received help and consideration from the unusually safe harbor that Stevens provided for those coming from the South.

A celebrated case that he won for James Dobbin placed Stevens squarely on the side of oppressed slaves. Dobbin won his freedom, and Stevens sheltered and supported him throughout the legal ordeal.

Another incident involved a proprietor of a local inn. Stevens had stopped by on his way to Philadelphia to purchase law books when he discovered that the owner of the inn, a Mr. Johnson, was attempting to sell a mulatto boy for $300. The boy was the man's son, and Stevens took all the money he had for books to buy the boy his freedom.

It was not unusual for the Stevens' residence to be a stopover on the trek north for many seeking freedom. He did so openly to the consternation of community leaders and editors. Dinah's ebullience added to the gossip around Gettysburg.

Over the summer, though, Dinah had grown sullen as it became clear that she was with child. She continued her daily walks to the Negro section of the town carrying her child and her secret with her. She did her duties at the Stevens residence and other households without fail.

Biographers know only the tragedy of Dinah. They are unsure of the circumstances surrounding her death and the impact it had on Thaddeus Stevens. Malicious editors from North and South would assert brazenly that Stevens committed the murder. They point out that his motive could easily have been political: Dinah could not be allowed to bear a child with the prominent (and white) characteristics of the Councilman. It was likely that the hereditary deformity of a withered limb would appear and prove that Stevens' interracial passions were more than rhetorical.

"Strange fits of passion have I known," wrote Wordsworth. The young lawyer from Gettysburg, the one who would lead the Radical Republicans and the nation into conflagration 40 years later, the "Old Commoner" who would influence Presidents and antagonize leaders North and South, the one who would most determine the direction of the nation based on fiery adherence to principle, developed that fire on a September night as he saw the crumpled, pregnant body of a young girl named Dinah at the bottom of a farmer's well on the outskirts of Gettysburg.

There are only two possibilities for the actions and results of that fateful day: either Stevens murdered his paramour to hide his paternity and became a prisoner to his guilt, or he was innocent and discovered the body of Dinah along with the passion that would motivate him entirely in years to come.

CHAPTER THREE

August 1823

Here is Dinah's story:

It was a hot August day 1823, on a small Emmitsburg, Maryland farm. The rocky, clay soil didn't yield its crops easily, and a handful of slaves scraped and hoed the fields, clearing the last stalks of corn, readying the ground for winter wheat planting. Some days when work was behind schedule, Thatcher would take up a hoe or a scythe and work alongside the team grumbling and cursing the "lazy coloreds." On hot days like this, though, he sat on the farm-house porch reading newspapers and smoking his long-curved pipe.

Charity Butler worked inside and would respond to his barks with ice water or sandwiches. She had just been returned to the farm and had resumed her household chores for her owner, Norman Bruce.

"I don't know why he puts up with you," Thatcher was saying. "I'd a whupped you good with one of those Georgia plantation bullwhips."

Charity looked at the sweaty, whiskered man on the rocking chair. He smelled like old coffee and sawdust and leered at her with twisted yellow teeth. Mister Bruce had made it clear that Charity was not to be touched, and Thatcher thoroughly resented her silent confidence.

It was almost dusk, and Thatcher had his gaze fixed on the young girl called Dinah. She was 17 or 18 and had grown firm on the farm. She never knew her father and, just six months ago, watched her mother carted away with hogs and chickens by two landowners from Virginia.

"It's just business," was all that Master Bruce had said.

Dinah put down the basket of stalks she was carrying and reached her long fingers down the small of her back. She arched far back, thrusting her breasts upward.

Thatcher's eyes narrowed, and Charity followed his stare to the girl as a thin smile, like a blade, crossed his face. "It's skinnin' time," he said.

"Bastard," Charity said aloud as she slammed the farmhouse door behind her.

Later in the large basin outside the barn, Charity soothed Dinah with warm water and gentle strokes of her long black hair. Dinah turned and pressed herself to Charity sobbing. "Why do they hurt us so?" Charity looked for a long time at the stars before answering: "No more child, no more."

A knock on his back door awakened Thaddeus Stevens. It was long after midnight, and he held an oil lamp to the face of the young black girl. The grime of her two-day journey matted her dress to her skin, and her hair hung like wet moss over her tired faced. Her eyes were moist and deep brown, and her frail beauty struck Stevens.

"Charity Butler sent me," Dinah said.

On the south side of town, at the foot of Cemetery Ridge, former slaves lived in clusters that approximated the families they once knew. Dinah moved in with an elderly couple who did subsistence farming and sewing for the shantytown. She had a "brother," known only as Black Peter, who was a huge, muscular man in his twenties with no schooling and no aptitude for it. Peter, who may have been slightly retarded, was the community blacksmith and could always be spotted in dirty overalls with one shoulder snap undone and no shirt underneath. He rarely wore shoes until the snow flew, and he always seemed to wear the smudged perspiration of his trade— whether he was before his furnace or out on the streets. Peter's affections for Dinah were unexpressed. Their hands never touched, and he rarely looked directly at her face on those mornings that he walked her up Washington to Chambersburg street to Master Hersh's or Master Stevens' house.

Dinah would often serve Master Stevens and Peter coffee after her chores at the Hersh house were finished. Often, Peter would leave the kitchen before Stevens arrived.

Dinah brought new life to the muddy lean-tos along Washington Street. She found herself in new clothes and warm surroundings for most of the days and spoke glowingly about the hours she spent in the Stevens household. Peter protected her from the hoodlums and the derelicts in the ghetto but worried more about her spending so much time in "the big houses."

What Dinah enjoyed best was the time spent in the library with Thaddeus Stevens. He read constantly and would read passages from Milton and Pope and Wordsworth aloud to her before a crackling fire. She, too, learned to read and spent long, pleasant hours undisturbed by memories in the room when Stevens was away on business. She normally returned to South Washington Street after the dinner was served, and the dishes were cleaned, and she brought her pleasant disposition with her. Most were brightened by her good fortune; others, still in various degrees of bondage, were clouded by envy or resentment; still others, like Peter, were just confused. ※

CHAPTER FOUR

January 1824

Thaddeus Stevens shook the snow from his black greatcoat as he escaped a cold night that reminded him of the stinging winters in Vermont. A brief, painful moment of childhood memories—his drunken father, his rough brothers, his overworked mother, schoolmasters, patronizing lawyers—and he resigned himself to another night alone.

But the fire was lit already, and the warmth was a welcome surprise. Dinah slept peacefully with her face pressed into the wing of the only chair in the library; her bare toffee-colored legs tucked snugly under her housedress. A volume of poetry spread upon the floor like a wounded bird.

Stevens had left after dinner for cards and Madeira with Jonathan Blanchard and others at the Gettysburg Hotel and was returning at midnight. He watched Dinah sleep for many minutes and smiled when she started, awake, and embarrassed.

"Oh," she said, "oh, I must be going."

Thaddeus reached to her and touched her for the first time. She watched as he watched her face. She followed him upstairs, where he left his loneliness inside of her. (Author's note: I wish I could take credit for this line. It comes from an American Haiku artist named George Swede.) (Van DenHeuvel, 1986, p. 236)

Months later, Jonathan Blanchard shook his head. He owed his legal education and his success in the Gettysburg community to Thaddeus. Stevens had been his mentor, and Blanchard was the closest thing Stevens had to a friend. Lately, Jonathan spent much time in his clerical role protecting Stevens from his indiscretions.

The community was still buzzing from his declamation on slavery of less than a year ago. Only a Borough councilman, Stevens was known for his abolitionist stance. His standing in the negro community grew with every kindness he extended to them and with every public action he took on their behalf. The question that had editors' eyebrows raised was: Why? What gave this neophyte politician the right or the gall to weigh in on an issue of such national proportions?

Like Stevens, Jonathan disdained the institution of slavery, but why make an issue of it here and now? Why jeopardize a promising legal and political future for such a cause? Why did he turn his home into a way station for these wretched types? And now this pregnant hand servant with the run of the house—what would people think?

"Should one human own another?" Stevens, back in his role as teacher, asked his former student.

"Of course not."

"Should one half of the economic system of this nation be based on labor from servitude? What chance do we have as a nation if our work product is based not on incentives but indenture?"

"But it is not your fight."

"Then," responded Thaddeus, "whose is it?"

"You know what the other lawyers say. You know what they think of you and Dinah."

"Suppose that you tell me, Jonathan."

Exasperated, Jonathan was as direct as he had ever been:

"You, they say are infatuated with a slave gi—"

"Former slave girl," Stevens interrupted.

"Former slave girl," Jonathan continued. "You, they say, have a personal interest in the abolitionist cause. You, they say, are a nigger lover."

"My, my," said Thad, "such erudition from my learned colleagues."

Jonathan, thinking of politics and his friend's potential on the local scene and, perhaps, Congress someday, protested:

"This is SERIOUS, Thad."

Stevens rose slowly and fixed his stare directly between his friend's eyes. Jonathan watched as Stevens' own eyes seemed to turn a deeper blue and then disappeared behind eyelids now as narrow as his razor straight mouth. It was the volcanic passion contained within that Jonathan had seen only once or twice before. It was a look that would strike fear into adversaries, one that demanded attention to the eruption about to occur.

"What is "serious" is ridding the nation of the infection of hatred. What is "serious" is freeing humans from chains and heart-break, from the most degrading condition imaginable—ownership by others who feel superior!" His voice was suddenly quiet:

"What is serious is grasping for a ray of happiness in this vale of tears—freeing oneself from the chains of loneliness."

He paused and looked away—somewhere beyond his focus, and before this time—he looked to a place in his childhood. After a long time, he quoted something his mother had said a long time ago: "Love, Jonathan, is all we have. It is the only way that each can help the other." Another pause. Then: "Dinah makes me smile. She carries my child."

Jonathan's mouth was round and wide open at the revelation: "My God, man, what will you do?"

"I will take her as my wife. I will raise the child as my offspring."

"You can't be serious."

"I am as serious as destiny itself," was his curious response. "I have already told her." ✻

CHAPTER FIVE

September 1824

Dinah walked briskly, her thin blue sweater opening like drapery on her enlarged stomach. She reached down to the lowest part of the curvature and felt the movement within and without. She wondered at the position and the strength of the little limbs. She would move into the big house. She would make a home for Thad and their child. She was as happy as she could ever remember being.

She had told her housemates and peers, not being able to contain the news. It was odd, she thought, that no one shared her joy. There was little approval, only world-weary clicking of tongues and the same, slow shaking of heads that she remembered when Thatcher would prey in the fields.

This, she knew, was different. Thad loved her. At least he treated her like that—she didn't expect to hear the words. She knew it was not going to be like a regular marriage—the local townsfolk would not tolerate a leading citizen in such a taboo liaison if it were flaunted. But they would be private and happy.

On a warm, Indian summer night, on September 23, 1824, Dinah was surprised to see Black Peter at the corner of Chambersburg and Washington streets. He must have seen Dinah and Thaddeus Stevens together as the dark cloaked-figure of Thaddeus Stevens was turning a corner moving toward the town square. He had just left her having explained that he had legal research to do, and Jonathan and others were coming to discuss the November Borough Council elections.

Peter looked down at her feet. This was not unusual because he had a difficult time looking at any person—white or black—in the eyes. What was unusual was that Dinah had not seen him for weeks. He had been leaving the blacksmith's shop earlier and earlier and went somewhere other than home on most evenings. On those rare occasions when his "family" saw him, they would ask where he'd been. "Walkin'" was all he would say.

On this evening, Peter reached clumsily for Dinah's hand and pulled her unexpectedly north on Washington Street in the direction of the Presbyterian church by the railroad tracks. He seemed troubled, and Dinah, though surprised by his forwardness, was content to join him as they walked past the small cemetery and the church on the flat land that would be the site of the Gettysburg/Lancaster rail line in the future. Peter, it seemed, liked following the path for miles. Years later, other townsfolk would step aside for the smoke-belching engine that carried Pennsylvania passengers to Lancaster and east and Chambersburg and west. This was the same train and the same tracks that would bring President Lincoln to town 39 years later.

They were heading toward the Freeman Farm. As Peter and Dinah walked behind the barn toward the wide, shallow well on the property, a hired hand lit a kerosene lamp in the bunkhouse. He watched as the two disappeared around the corner and then later saw Peter close to the "mud-hole" in the gathering gloom of nightfall.

The farmhand, a man named David Fletcher, made a nightly round of the grounds and lowered his lantern as deeply as he could reach into the well. There was no question about it, he thought, it was Councilman Stevens' housekeeper. She was from the other end of town, but all of Gettysburg knew about the pregnant mulatto who traipsed around like she "owned the place." The farmhand found her pleasant and helpful when he had encountered her at the market or the square, but he knew to keep a distance and was not above sharing in some rumor-mongering. Perhaps because of her past kindnesses, perhaps as a sort of penance for his part in the town's gossip, he felt obliged to climb the short hill to Chambersburg Street to inform the Councilman.

Others had seen the two coloreds near the farm and had speculated about them wandering on the wrong side of town. Some had seen the farmhand's lantern at twilight in the well, and, by the time Thaddeus Stevens arrived, a small crowd had gathered around the stone mouth of the well. ❋

———

Later, in a legal proceeding (Stevens v. LeFever) both Fletcher and a Mr. William McPherson, a prominent local banker would recall that evening. Some sketchy notes from Fletcher's recollections at that trial:

> . . . [there was] a group of men standing by . . . When Peter observed them . . . he remarked to Wm. [McPherson]: "Wonder what these men are doing there—I bet they found a dead negro . . ." Bill let us go and see what they are about—they turned back till they come to North Street— there they met Mrs. Gilland and McP . . . Peter asked her: "Have they found Dinah?" (see notes of defense counsel Stevens v. LeFever).

———

Stevens arrived in a long, black solicitor's coat and crepe ribbon tied tightly at the neck, having just completed a day in the court-house and at his office. He was winded because he had dragged his club foot behind the rest of his body and had lunged over the short hill in a strenuous clumping gait that announced his presence on the scene. The townsfolk parted whispering at the well like nervous geese. They all wanted to see what would happen next. ❋

———

Other incidents in the young lawyer's life seemed strange precursors to this evening's events. Other deaths haunted him. There was the carnage of the spotted fever outbreak back in Vermont; and there was the unfortunate suicide of the recently freed slave, Keziah just four years earlier right in his home. Mrs. O'Neill was the large Negro guardian of the Stevens household in 1820, and it was she who cut Keziah's dead body down from the attic rafters. Keziah, like many caught in the harsh politics of the time, could find no life in the north or the south. She had been freed but would be a prisoner of her confusion until she found her special rite of passage.

Even then, there were rumblings about Stevens' involvement that stemmed from racial malice and political treachery. Keziah was a child of 15 who received room and board from Stevens and hope from Mrs. O'Neill. It was Mrs. O'Neill who exonerated Stevens of any wrongdoing. She told authorities at the time that Master Stevens was too generous for his own good. Biographer Elsie Singmaster would write later that "dark-skinned creatures on their way north applied at Mr. Stevens' door." (Singmaster, n.d., p. 182)

Tonight, Stevens faced his destiny at the bottom of the mud-hole well. Tonight, Dinah and the child were brutally removed from any role in his future. Except for the constant innuendo and the occasional overt murder charge that would follow him, Stevens was utterly alone again.

An unswerving dedication to the cause of the slave and the oppressed, which sprang from this well and other incidents throughout his private and public life would condemn Stevens to never-ending criticism. He would assume a pivotal role in the shaping of a country in turmoil but would be denied historic rank among lesser figures because of the mystery of Dinah, a woman named Lydia Smith, and the darkness of his loneliness. ✳

Late in his career, Jeremiah Black, a political enemy in the cabinet of President Buchanan, would remark that the mind of Thaddeus Stevens "as far as its obligation to God was concerned, was a howling wilderness." (Korngold, 1955, p. 11)

Stevens watched his townsfolk shake their heads slowly and cast an occasional glance in his direction. He also saw Black Peter heading due west on the pathway toward Chambersburg, never to be seen in Gettysburg again. He headed back toward 51 Chambersburg Street aware of the stares of the townspeople on his back. His home seemed large, cold, and beast-like as he turned the key and entered.

Stevens crumpled in pain when he was at last alone. He found himself sobbing and, oddly, moaning unconsciously. Then, in his present wilderness, he uttered a brief actual howl at the nightmare of the crumpled, bloodied Dinah. He moved slowly into the library but did not bother setting the fireplace. He leaned forward in his chair, holding his head with both hands. "What now?" he thought.

He decided to visit with his private counsel, Jonathan Blanchard. He would see him on Sunday, even if it meant sitting through his church service.

On Sunday mornings, the young Reverend Jonathan Blanchard climbed the creaky steps to the bell tower of the Presbyterian Church. Before he reached for the thick rope that would rock the cast iron bell summoning worshipers to the morning service, he would spend a few moments in quiet meditation surveying the soft hills and valleys surrounding Gettysburg. It was his regular Sunday ritual.

Across the meadow to the north stood a white stucco building as a center of worship and education. It was the only center of higher learning between Baltimore and Harrisburg, and the Lutherans had the presumption to name their three-story, twelve-room school-house the Pennsylvania College. It would grow in time to become Gettysburg College while both the Presbyterian Church and its small adjacent cemetery would make way for a spur of the Chambersburg to Harrisburg rail line.

From his perch, Jonathan could see over the rise to the main part of Gettysburg where the hotel, several pubs and boarding houses, and the courthouse defined a neatly maintained square that served as a crossroads for horse and wagon traffic heading to all parts of Pennsylvania and the border of Maryland and the southern states.

Seminary Ridge lay beyond the fields to the north. It was already a center for theology and for training the Lutheran ministers who taught at the College. In the other direction, traveling due south on Washington street, Jonathan looked over the shanties of the black section of town and followed the rills and pastures beyond to the point where they lapped up against Cemetery Ridge. The lush forests on all the hillsides were laced with light greens and yellows as they were becoming autumn's canvas.

The serenity of Gettysburg's hills and valleys comforted Jonathan. He and his church sat in a verdant bowl that would be stirred to a furious tempest in a battle that would change the world thirty-nine years later.

Even today, in the splendor of this Sunday morning, there was a specter of death. Less than a mile to the west of the church, within clear view of the young preacher sitting in his steeple, was the Freeman farm. Jonathan could see clear to the bottom of the well by the barn. He shook his head.

Dinah, the mulatto house servant of his friend and teacher, Thaddeus Stevens, had been murdered three days before. Her body, pregnant and crumpled at the bottom of the well, was severely bruised with a dark blue contusion visible on her forehead. "So young," thought Jonathan.

In the Negro section of town, there would be no Sunday services. Most of the inhabitants along South Washington Street were Baptists and transplants from the cotton and wheat fields of the south. They had found their way to Gettysburg and to strange new freedom that offered little more than menial, backbreaking chores that left little time for amenities like building a church or a congregation.

Instead of a chapel, families or remnants of families would gather at each other's homes and sing the spirituals that their parents had taught them years before. They sang "Amazing Grace" and "All My Trials." They sang the sad, sweaty songs of the field.

They sang of oppression and the thin hope of real deliverance. But there was no mention of Dinah in any of these clusters today.

A vibrant, attractive girl who smiled with strong, perfect teeth, she had lived with her foster "family" and had found a pleasant position in the home of one of Gettysburg's most prominent citizens and did work in several other households. She was fed and clothed well above the ghetto standard and was the object of some envy among her own. A warm girl, Dinah was especially exuberant on the night before her death. Her pregnancy didn't seem to trouble her; she was elated. She had found her kind of deliverance and had confided to one or two in her community that she and her child would soon be living in the "big house" on Chambersburg Street.

Her joy went unrequited. She was confused by the resentment she felt from her peers. Today, there was no eulogy. There was only emptiness in the spot that Dinah filled. Her closest friend, Peter, had also disappeared. Gettysburg was without its blacksmith.

Jonathan Blanchard grasped the thick, coiled cord and tugged mightily. The bell sounded its long, sad tone and lifted the preacher off the ground with each swing. Blanchard gave one final pull and brushed off his hands.

Robed and in the pulpit, the young Reverend Jonathan Blanchard was striking. His hair was jet black and so straight and disciplined that it seemed to frame his whole being. Sharp lines at his cheeks and the thin, sturdy frame that he carried like an athlete gave him an aura of strength that he put to good use when he preached. A bit young for the fire and brimstone of the Lutheran elders across the way, he nevertheless delivered energetic homilies that dipped into his considerable knowledge of the Bible, the Classics, and the events of the day.

For his religious muse, he summoned up the firebrand writings of Jonathan Edwards. For his literary references and political acumen, he could thank the private tutoring of Thaddeus Stevens. As a very young man, he studied law with Stevens under the learned Judge William Mattock. The jurist saw the spark in both men and was pleased to guide "one toward the Lord and the other toward the law." It was Stevens who read voraciously and who would pass along his literary discoveries to Jonathan.

But it was Jonathan who emerged from childhood and adolescence with grace and religious fervor; not the cynicism and pragmatism that would teem from the "darkly wise" Stevens. Indeed, theirs was an odd friendship that townsfolk found disconcerting. Though some knew him for generous acts and remarkable courage, Stevens was maligned by many as petulant, angry, and godless. Blanchard was bright and good. Stevens was severe. Together they formed an alliance of qualities that would help them both through life's challenges. Jonathan, well-loved and beyond reproach, graced the Gettysburg community with his presence. Stevens was far too brusque and calculating to trust in conviviality. He had colleagues and confidants, but Jonathan Blanchard was his only friend.

Jonathan, resplendent, was startled to see the black over-coated figure of Thaddeus Stevens sitting in the back row of his church. In the five years he had been pastor, this was the first appearance of his murky friend in his church, or, thought Jonathan, ANY church for that matter. It was, however, the second time in a week that Stevens had been in this part of town. He was there when it happened.

Stevens waited in the quiet, lonely way that was his own. The congregation waited for a while, and the children began to fidget. Jonathan Blanchard collected his thoughts and prepared to offer a Bible lesson that would comfort and inspire his friend. He hoped Stevens would listen.

From Nehemiah, Chapter 2:

"And it came to pass in the month of Nisanin the twentieth year of Artaxerxes the king, that wine was before him: and I took up the wine and gave it unto the king. Now I had not been beforetime sad in his presence.

Wherefore the king said unto me, Why is thy countenance sad, seeing thou are not sick? This is nothing but sorrow of heart. Then I was very sore afraid,

And said unto the king, Let the king live forever: why should not my countenance be sad when the city, the place Of my fathers' sepulchres, lieth waste and the gates thereof are consumed with fire?

Then the king said unto me, For what dost thou make request? So I prayed to the God of heaven.

And I said unto the king, If it please the king, and if thy servant have found favour in thy sight, that thou wouldest send me unto Judah, unto the city of my fathers' sepulchres, that I may build it.

And the king said unto me, (the queen sitting by him,) For how long shall thy journey be? and when wilt thou return? So it pleased the king to send me; and I set him a time.

Moreover, I said unto the king, If it please the king, let letters be given me to the governors beyond the river, that they may convey me over till I come into Judah.

And a letter unto Asaph the keeper of the king's forest, that he may give me timber to make beams for the gates of the palace which appertained to the house, and for the wall of the city, and for the house that I shall enter into. And the king granted me, according to the good hand of my God upon me.

Then I came to the governors beyond the river and gave them the king's letters. Now the king had sent captains of the army and horsemen with me.

When Sanballat the Horonite, and Tobiah the servant, the Ammonite heard of it, it grieved them exceedingly that there was come a man to seek the welfare of the children of Israel.

So I came to Jerusalem, and was there three days."

Jonathan Blanchard shone brightly when he preached the Word. "Nehemiah was sore afraid in the presence of his king. He was, after all, the wine-bearer, the hand-servant. He was not an advisor or a noble. He came into the king's presence only to serve. To provide the cup to the royal couple. But the king was quick to notice the sadness in his servant's heart: 'Why is thy countenance sad?'"

At this, Stevens shifted in the back row, and Jonathan knew he was listening even though his countenance was bowed.

"And it was Nehemiah who was smart enough to make a request: 'send me to Judah' that I may rebuild the walls of Jerusalem, that I may restore the city of my ancestors to its proper glory.

"The king made way for Nehemiah. He provided transport and safe passage. He gave him the provisions and the political support he needed to travel freely and to obtain the timber to build. But it was GOD (and here Jonathan reared back to roar his emphasis) who had put in Nehemiah's heart what to do at Jerusalem. It was GOD who guided the entire mission. It was GOD who led Nehemiah and his king on their journeys.

"And it was mere men who stood in the way. Nehemiah encountered those who despised the children of Israel along the way. Despite his divine calling, despite authorization from the king, there are still enemies who presume to distract us from our purpose.

"So I came to Jerusalem and was there three days."

And the lesson from Pastor Blanchard:

"Nehemiah says he told no man "what God had put in his heart." He alone knew the power and the meaning and the purpose. He came with the might of the Almighty inside of him and was made to simmer for three days that surely seemed like an eternity.

For when the vision is revealed (Jonathan in rising tones again), it must not be denied. When we have building to do according to the Almighty Architect, we must be about His business. The distractions of this life must not deter us from our destiny. There is pain, there is sorrow, there is opposition, but there is a reason for the vision, and its fulfillment is demanded by our God.

As we face our challenges, as we encounter pain and temptations, remember this is but the meantime. We are living in that uncomfortable period between the revelation of the vision and the fulfillment of the vision. In this meantime, whether it be three days in Jerusalem or thirty years in Gettysburg, let us be strong. Let us cling to the vision so that we can build when our meantime is over."

Here, Jonathan looked straight at the dark figure and was startled to see Thaddeus Stevens staring straight back. He quoted the Bible like he was making a legal case:

"Isaiah, Chapter 10, Verse 6: 'I will send him against a hypocritical nation.'

"Isaiah, Chapter 11, Verse 4: 'But with righteousness shall he judge the poor and reprove with equity the meek of the earth: and he shall smite the earth with the rod of his mouth, and with the breath of his lips shall stay the wicked.'"

The words connected the preacher and his congregation of one like a beam of light. Townsfolk who did not understand looked, nevertheless, from one man to the other as if expecting some further revelation. In those eternal seconds, the mind of Thaddeus Stevens was racing with emotions.

There would be a Coroner's inquest. There would be suspicion—even accusations. He would deal with the situation. What he was feeling now, though, was a hot knife slicing through his chest, a memory that was so fresh that it seemed more real than the hard, cold pew of the church on which he found himself. He remembered Dinah turning for one last parting glance as she headed toward Washington Street, and he toward his home on Chambersburg. She was smiling as she patted the lower portion of her swollen stomach. He smiled back, but she could see the confusion in his eyes.

Yes, he had told her they would be a family. But even he had no idea of how to proceed. It would not do to move mother and child directly in. She was, after all, an employee of Mr. George Hersh and worked only occasionally for Stevens. It would be a brazen admission of interracial paternity that would surely wreck his Council career and any other aspirations. He, of course, had arranged her employment shortly after she presented herself on his back doorstep two years ago. She said she was referred by Charity Butler and Stevens felt obliged—even eager—to provide for her in the face of the Fugitive Slave law, which he found repugnant.

As for George Hersh, he was a prominent businessman who provided a subsistence wage to Dinah for household chores as young Thaddeus' income was subject to payment from clients for legal work that was intermittent at best. Hersh was generous to Dinah and allowed her to tend to Stevens as well. Like most townsfolk, he had his suspicions regarding the type of services rendered but said nothing to Stevens. ✻

––––––––

While he was not a gregarious sort, Stevens attended several functions at George Hersh's home. The last event was a celebratory round of toasts on the Fourth of July 1823. After the town reading of the Declaration of Independence, the ladies and gentlemen of the town heard from Doctor C. N. Berlucchy, who orated for an hour on the courthouse steps. The gentlemen retired to Hersh's house and, following the traditional reading of President George Washington's farewell address, the toasts began.

Stevens was the first to inject politics into the proceedings by toasting "the next President: may he be a freeman, who never riveted fetters on a human slave." Others saluted the current President and Governor, the Constitution, and the exploits of Bolivar in South America. Dinah moved quietly and quickly among the men, filling glasses and averting gazes. She was even more attractive than when she appeared that first night in the rain, thought Stevens and his assessment of her was shared by the admiring group.

She allowed herself a trace of a smile when Stevens stared and refused to look away. It was then that he rose a second time to offer an unusual toast of gratitude to the day's speaker: "A chaste scholar and an unassuming citizen." What chastity had to do with the lecture escaped the others. Dinah scurried into the kitchen. (see The Centinel, July 9, 1823).

In their private moments together, Stevens said he loved her. Yes, he had uttered those words to her. It was the first time he had ever used the expression except with his mother, Sarah. Dinah believed he loved her. Stevens believed that he wanted to love her. It was, of course, completely unacceptable and yet, the most honorable thing he could do.

On the evening of Dinah's death, his left leg was throbbing, but he kept walking toward the hotel. He needed company, reassurance. Maybe some colleagues or Jonathan would be at the Hotel. He glanced back one last time to see Dinah turning right toward the church and Freeman's farm; not left toward the shanties on Washington Street. He was concerned until he recognized Peter and heard Dinah's little laugh. They were like brother and sister. She would be all right. ✻

Here is how the *Gettysburg Compiler* recorded the incident in their September 29, 1824, edition:

SHOCKING OCCURENCE

On Friday last, the dead body of a colored female, who had resided with Mr. George Hersh of this borough was found in an old well, in West Street. The Coroner's inquest, we understand, reported that she was found drowned, from causes unknown. This is an extraordinary case: The water did not exceed three feet in depth, in the middle, (and the sides were sloping) in which she lay with her face downwards—and, as she had a bruise on one of her temples, the opinion appears to be pretty general that she was the object of a most deliberate murder. The suspicion is strengthened by the fact of her having been in an advanced state of pregnancy.

He had been at the well. He saw her crumpled in the water. He saw David Fletcher and the farmhands lower the thinnest one down to attach the rope to retrieve her body. He left as the crowd continued to gather and followed his stunned automatic footsteps home. The stone house before him stood like a monument, a mausoleum. It stood stoically in the face of his predicament and seemed to elongate to a distorted carnival mirror size. He would be swallowed up by the front door and enter the insatiable mouth of his loneliness. How often had he pranced through that door after an afternoon with Dinah? How often had he wondered about the possibility of moving her in—for better and worse—like a real family?

There was no need to wonder anymore. She was gone. ❦

The *Centinel* was the first to cast doubt on the coroner's jury findings:

"A coroner's inquest was called, who reported that she came to her death by drowning but in a manner unknown to the jury. Every circumstance is in contradiction to the idea of its being accidental; and the generally received opinion is, that violent hands were laid on her. There was but one mark of violence, which was near the right eye, and when opened, a considerable quantity of extravasated blood was found there. This leads to the suspicion, that if she has been murdered, a blow was given on the temple, and her immediately thrown into the water, where she was drowned, before she could recover her senses. She was very far advanced in pregnancy." (*Centinel*, September 29, 1824)

The article and the proceedings infuriated Stevens. He sat on the panel and heard Miss Emma McPherson, the daughter of his banker friend, point to the "muddy shirt" that the usually fastidious Stevens was wearing that night. He heard a Mr. John Gavin say that Stevens suspected him of "knowing too much" and, he swore, sometime in the confusion of the evening that Stevens had fired a pistol at him. Someone presented testimony that a Mr. James Dobbins's gun was missing and, with his trial only recently completed, suspicious eyes turned to Dobbins's defense counsel—Thaddeus Stevens. Several weeks after the jury's pronouncement, the gun would be found in Stevens' closet "still loaded with two balls" Stevens scowled. Here, again, Stevens viewed himself as a victim of his kindness. He had won freedom for the former slave both from the trumped-up charges of a vindictive former owner and from servitude itself. More, he had supplied room and board for Dobbins throughout the trial. It was a proud moment for Dobbins when he could finally purchase a firearm as a free man, and he stored it in one of Stevens' closets.

Martha Hersh, daughter of his friend George, said bluntly: "the whole family knows Stevens was out late that night." It was Stevens who suggested raising a substantial sum for a reward, but another panelist, John McFarlane scoffed at the suggestion saying, "it would be folly to pretend there was not a suspicion in the matter." At this, Stevens had had enough and left the jury to its counsel and purposes. They came to no conclusion or indictment, but it would not be the last time that Stevens would face suspicion for the deed.

A rehash of the entire incident would be at the core of a libel case brought by Stevens after repeated published innuendos by his powerful peers. That case was to end equally ambiguously in August 1833. Stevens viewed the accusers as cowards and enemies who sought to derail his political ambitions.

But on the night of the murder, there was not hatred but pain. There arose an alien sound, a faint moan like that of a dying man from somewhere in the street. It was a terrifying noise that was oddly reassuring in its purring cadence. It was the tense rugged murmur of rampaging passions held inside the belly of some great beast. The noise grew louder. It filled his head. When he discovered that the groaning was escaping from his lips, he found himself sobbing, then wailing, then actually howling, then shaking. It was not

the first time he felt abandoned; it would not be the last time that
he stood with fists punching wildly at the unknown.

This boxing match with the Deity had him bleeding badly, though
he had worked hard and expected at least a fair fight. He felt suddenly miserably mortal; he had been presumptuous enough to think
that he could earn his way back to his vision and cleanse himself
of the imperfections that dogged him just as his clumsy, deformed
foot dragged along when he walked. But there was only darkness
that night. He stood alone again, with dashed hopes reopening the
wounds of his sacrifices.

And so, it was that he found himself in Jonathan's church. What
did he expect to find? Comfort? Understanding? Absolution?

He sat looking straight ahead, not returning the glances of the
townsfolk who filed past on their way out of the church. Jonathan
greeted his congregation outside in his usual fashion and returned to
sit with his friend.

"Is there something for you to confess?" he asked gently but
directly.

Thaddeus Stevens said nothing. He gathered his greatcoat
around his shoulders and strode out the door.

———

Thaddeus Stevens sat bolt upright in the wing chair of his
library in the house on Chambersburg Street. Collar fastened, vest
buttoned, and black suit covering his bony frame like a blanket of
darkness, he sat with the formality of a corpse. His bony fingers
were spread wide on his knees, and the only movement in the
House was from the shadows that crept on to the bookcases and
mantelpiece as the afternoon turned into evening. Stevens had the
look of a man somberly awaiting an unwanted guest, and he had
been staring forward in that condition since he had returned from
Jonathan's church.

He had not attended the internment services, such as they were,
for Dinah. Shock and horror at the sight of her crumpled body inside
the earth in the well was the silent elegy that he would carry with

him from this day forward. There was no eulogy at her gravesite, just another lowering of another colored girl who paid the price of her presumption. A few old negroes who came out of some sense of community obligation had walked away, shaking their heads.

It would have sickened Stevens to see not outrage but subjugation among the colored faces who comprised her "family." There was no rage about the brutality of the crime, more a resignation about the ultimate end of servitude. Indeed, circumstances for blacks in the fields of Maryland or the shanties of Gettysburg were harsh enough to make death almost welcome. So there was no chorus singing the tragedy of Dinah—only blank numbness like children staring out at the vastness of space abandoned by a universe that had made freedom as distant as the stars.

Stevens, too, began to feel a physical numbness. The tingling began in his fingertips and an odd thickness of his tongue. He was cold and hungry and yet felt the beginnings of fever like tiny pinpricks all over his skin. Suddenly, he felt incapable of speech or movement. He closed his eyes, and on the back of his eyelids danced a furious display of reds and yellows as he watched the misfirings of the synapses in his brain. Then there was darkness with a cloudlike ball of light swirling in the distance. It began to move closer, taking on a variety of shapes like smoke from a campfire. Then it had a face—a child's face—a baby squinting with unbearable pain. He had seen that face before on a cold winter night in Vermont. He watched as the formal struggle against the pain relaxed and surrendered to the night.

Then a dark, shining face. A fresh face with luminescent teeth that bestowed her smile like a gift. Ringlets of freshly curled brown hair made the young girl look almost comically innocent. "Keziah," thought Stevens as he reached for her. At that moment, the vision changed. The bright face was suddenly gray, tilted grotesquely to the left with a rope burning into her neck.

And suddenly, a new image as the cloud became dark as midnight with flashes of light and rolling thunder. The new face

appeared as a huge, looming ghost—Dinah in all her avatars. Dinah
the lost, soaking wet puppy on his doorstep seeking only comfort.
Dinah, the child, curled up in his library abandoning the struggle for
knowledge temporarily to give way to sleep. Dinah, the strong mistress of the house who filled the place with her movements whether
she was cooking, cleaning, or tending to the occasional visitors who
would stop by to discuss law and politics.

Then, larger than imagination itself, appeared the closed eyes
and bruised head lying in the abyss, painting the bottom of the well
wretched rust with her blood.

How long did the visions go on? Seconds? Minutes? Hours?
He was burning up, and the images danced and licked at him like
tongues of fire. He thought that he would soon join the dead. ✻

PART TWO

The Passion

CHAPTER SIX

December 1824

Strange fits of passion have I known:
And I will dare to tell,
But in the Lover's ear alone,
What once to me befell.
    When she I loved looked every day
    Fresh as a rose in June,
    I to her cottage bent my way,
    Beneath an evening moon.
Upon the moon, I fixed my eye,
All over the wide lea;
With quickening pace, my horse drew nigh
Those paths so dear to me.
    And now we reached the orchard plot;
    And, as we climbed the hill,
    The sinking moon to Lucy's cot
    Came near and nearer still.
In one of those sweet dreams, I slept,
Kind Nature's gentlest boon!
And all the while my eyes I kept
On the descending moon.
    My horse moved on; hoof after hoof
    He raised, and never stopped:

When down behind the cottage roof,
    At once, the bright moon dropped.
What fond and wayward thoughts will slide
Into a Lover's head!
"O mercy!" to myself I cried,
"If Lucy should be dead!"
(Abrams, *Norton Anthology*, Wordsworth, p. 113)

From the Gettysburg Compiler, December 8, 1824:

Mr. LeFever:

Some weeks ago, I was in Gettysburg, where the inhabitants appeared
to be much agitated, on account of a colored girl that had been found
dead, in an old well, in one of the back streets of the town. At every
corner as I passed thro' the streets, I saw groups standing conversing
upon the subject; and wherever I stop to listen to the conversations,
the universal opinion was, that she had been murdered by some
person—but no name was mentioned on whom the suspicion rested:
yet there were so many hints given as led me to believe that there were
sufficient grounds to suspect one person.

Having occasion to be in Gettysburg at the last court, I had an
expectation, from the conversations I had heard, that I should see
someone brought before the court, on a charge of having committed the fact. But, seeing nothing of that kind, and not hearing it,
anything of the matter which so much engaged the attention of
the inhabitants a few weeks before, I was led to believe that they
had found their former suspicions were ill-founded and that the
girl had done the violence herself, which had caused her death: but
upon inquiring at some conversing on the subject, I found they still
retained the same opinions, and that nothing had been brought to
light that had in the least weakened their former suspicions. Of those
I had heard speak of the disastrous affair formerly, I found they had
almost forgotten that such an occurrence had taken place; yet, upon
inquest, I understood, had said was begotten by a white man . . .

In other places, where even suspicion, as strong as has been evidenced by the inhabitants of Gettysburg, has existed, the constituted authorities have been prompt in taking the most efficient measures to discover the guilty perpetrators of such gross violation of the laws of both God and man . . . —Philanthropist

From the *Gettysburg Compiler,* December 29, 1824:

Mr. LeFever:
From a publication I saw, lately, in your paper, together with common fame, I find there is some person in your place, strongly suspected of being guilty of the murder of the colored girl spoken of. If it would not be inconsistent with your duty as an Editor and would be attended with no risk of a prosecution, I would be much obliged to you if you would give to the public the name of the person against whom the suspicion rests . . . if I comprehend this case aright, the suspected person, in committing the fact, has, in consequence, destroyed his own innocent offspring. —Caesar

December 31, 1824

Thaddeus Stevens sat alone in his office on New Year's Eve, 1824. The latest edition of *The Compiler* drooped like a dead leaf from his hand. The newspaper and its editor, Jacob LeFever, were not about to let the matter of Dinah rest. His legal training told him that they had carefully avoided a slanderous direct mention of his name, but his political sense jangled at the thought of a continued barrage of printed innuendo. The inquest had dissolved without complete resolution, and the matter had been dropped. No one was implicated, and no one was cleared.

"Philanthropist, Caesar, indeed," Stevens muttered. He knew that the writer and the editor were the same. Jacob LeFever was too cowardly to affix his name to the articles but could accomplish his backhanded assault on Stevens effectively. There was no counterpoint. At this moment, Stevens had three thoughts: the local paper and LeFever would be unrelenting in their opposition to his fledgling political career. It was political and personal. Stevens had just gotten re-elected to the Gettysburg Council in November and had shown "radical" leanings even in his first term in first elected office. His anti-slavery speeches in 1823 seemed to LeFever and other northern editors unnecessarily incendiary. For all their public hubris, the editors were content to abide by the "peculiar institution" because they feared the consequences of abolition. And, thought LeFever and the complacent: why stir this up here? In Gettysburg? On a town council? Stevens looked dangerous or at least bothersome, and he would be watched.

This led Stevens to a second thought that was only fleeting for now: he must find an outlet for his positions. Doing battle with a man who has an unlimited supply of ink would be futile. If his legal and business interests grew, he determined to give serious thought to investing in his newspaper. He could be as influential and manipulative as LeFever, and it would be for good causes; not gossip. It would rise like a star over Gettysburg and proclaim the truth as Stevens saw it like a banner. Someday.

The third thought was of Dinah. He had allowed himself the pleasure of passion for the first time in his life. He gave and took with the abandon a lover and felt an odd betrayal by her death. He vowed that he would never get too close to the fire again. He would retreat to his books and his speeches and his causes. They would be his passion. He would do what he had to do alone.

Stevens had felt the stares of the townsfolk and new of their suspicions. Perhaps he had been too public with Dinah. Perhaps he had offended the sensitivities of the gentry—particularly the pompous editor of the Compiler, who published only tepid articles on race and the slavery question. It offended Stevens mightily that the murder was being used to highlight the real "crime" he committed against this hypocritical society—consortium with a colored girl. ✻

———

There would be more articles and more rumors. LeFever's paper would be more and more creative in pointing to Stevens without falling over the precipice of libel. A "colloquium" between a "townsman" and a "countryman" gossiped about hush money to a particular witness and "a universal opinion of guilt . . . against an individual . . . walking the streets, in broad daylight, with his hands . . . streaming with human blood." In February 1825, LeFever was growing even less subtle:

To bring the subject home to the feelings of everyone, let us suppose, that any one of our most reputable citizens, (a clergyman, or a respectable mechanic, for example) had been . . . assassinated—would the matter be suffered to rest for five or six months . . . without any attempt to discover the assassin? We believe not.

For the midnight murderer of his own offspring (if such a one resides amongst us,) would not hesitate to imbrue his hand in the blood of any other person.

And yet another "colloquium" published this exchange in March:

COUNTRYMAN: This matter seems to be such a common topic of conversation in town, that I wonder it has not reached the ears of the suspected person.
TOWNSMAN: I have no doubt that it has. The subject is spoken of with so little reserve in families, that even the children have come to the knowledge of it. For, one day, when the person suspected passed where several them were at play, one of them, in a low voice, says to his companion—"I don't see any blood on that fellow's hands, as Mother said there was.

The Compiler and LeFever would go to some unusual lengths to inject the subject into other articles. The unrelated murder of a young girl in Maryland prompted this comment in May 1825:

It is doubtful, however, whether the above-mentioned crime was more inhuman than the one committed in this Borough on the night of September 23rd of September last; yet our honorable Burgess and

Town Council could not be prevailed upon to offer a reward . . .
Neither, we believe, has our neighbor of the Centinel noticed the
subject since the 29th of September last.

Indeed, the Centinel, the more anti-slavery, Jeffersonian-Democrat
paper, had applauded Stevens' early statements as an elected official and
had written only of the facts of the Dinah murder. But Stevens knew that
he would get little comfort from that quarter. Again, the thought of a
new outlet was creeping into his mind.

The July 1826 article would be the snidest:

Suppose a man to have destroyed the life of a colored female, while in
a state of pregnancy by him; suppose him to be unmarried, who, in his
criminal intercourse with the opposite sex, makes mistress, maid, and
colored females, the indiscriminate objects of his seductive practices;
suppose, too, that he is a gambler, who has essentially contributed to
ruin several men, who were doing good business for the support of
themselves and families; Could, or ought, such a state of things exist, in
the present state of society, without our special wonder and surprise?

Even before the barrage of articles that would appear in the new
year, Stevens cursed the cowardice. "Just come out with it,"
he thought. He knew enough of politics to expect attacks, but he
needed enough of a weapon to counter-punch. He would wait for five
years before a renewed attack on the same subject, and an entirely
different issue would give him a chance.

In the meantime, Thaddeus Stevens settled into the new year
with other things on his mind. He would concentrate on his invest-
ments and his law practice. He was very much interested in the
iron industry and knew that railroads could be lucrative markets
for the forged rails that could be produced with the resources and
labor available in south-central Pennsylvania. He was accumulating
property and building his private resources for what was to come. ✺

CHAPTER SEVEN

September 1826

Two years after Dinah's death, it was unusually mild in Gettysburg. Perhaps affected by the weather, Thaddeus Stevens allowed himself the rare plea-sure of company and sat with his few close friends at cards at his home several doors down from the town square. The bout with typhoid had left him bald, and he covered his scarred skull with a coal-black wig unless he was alone. He still had the piercing steel-blue eyes and the sardonic wit for which he had grown famous in the courtroom or at the card table. But social gatherings of any type were rare exceptions in his hard life.

Stevens, still serving as a Gettysburg Councilman, had thrown him-self into business and political activities. He was appointed a Director of the prestigious Gettysburg Bank and invested in a partnership to buy and operate the Maria Furnace, an iron manufacturing facility with hopes of supplying the burgeoning railroad industry in Pennsylvania and across the country.

Given the incessant attacks he received from journalists and rivals in those early days, he derived sardonic pleasure in founding his newspaper, the *Star and Banner*. He would use it to publish his speeches and to counterpunch in print.

Still, there had been little joy in his life since the loss of Dinah. Death and sadness hung like saddle-weights on him. A young, talented lawyer who should have been enjoying his growing prominence and prosperity, Stevens instead felt a constant burden. He still had the fiery determination to succeed; to swim against the tide of wrong that he saw everywhere, but incidents in his life continued to pull him under the surface.

Since Dinah, there had been the incident with James, the Gettysburg bank cashier who left the Stevens' home and its well-stocked wine cellar more inebriated than any of his cronies thought. A "commoner" like Thaddeus, he had befriended Stevens at the bank and was an occasional visitor to the card games. Word arrived that he had been found dead the morning after imbibing with the card players. Thaddeus anguished.

Then he raged for James and against injustice—his nemesis. He took an ax to every bottle and jug in his basement and swore off strong drink forever.

Lame William Thompson, who now sat directly across from him at the card table, stabbed another memory into him. Because of Thaddeus Stevens' kindness to him as a result of their shared deformity, William Thompson had named his son Thaddeus. Stevens was proud and protective of the boy, right up to the moment that he died in a drowning accident in a lake near Gettysburg.

Another card mate who was not present that evening was a prominent doctor who regularly received "anonymous" fees from Stevens to treat indigent handicapped children. Dr. Pfeiffer also had a son named Thaddeus. In the web of fate that Stevens' himself would help spin; Thaddeus Stevens Pfeiffer would be killed at the battle of Cold Harbor during the Civil War.

Death had been a dense and lumbering presence since his earliest days. He brooded about Vermont, Keziah, James, Charity Butler, and Dinah. He had been as Frost would say, "acquainted with the night." So, it was unusual that his young friend, Jonathan Blanchard, who sat in his usual place to the right of Thaddeus at the card table would suggest another morbid incident not as a millstone but as an opportunity.

On September 11, 1826, William Morgan, a bricklayer from Batavia, New York, was kidnapped and driven by carriage toward Fort Niagara at what observers said was "break-neck speed." He was never heard from again.

William Morgan had antagonized the growing Masonic Order by committing the unpardonable sin. He wrote a book about the secrets and rituals of the movement. Already a subject of skepticism from those who questioned the mystic nature of the organization and its selective membership rules, anti-masons were convinced that Morgan's murder was no accident.

Even though prominent men like Henry Clay, Andrew Jackson, and most of the founding fathers had belonged to the order, church groups had branded Freemasonry "unfit" for Christians. The Mennonites, Amish, Quakers, and other sects in central Pennsylvania were especially dubious of this mystic cult.

Thurlow Reed, the New York publisher, had attacked the Masons repeatedly, and his account of the Morgan murder was the topic that Jonathan Blanchard brought up this evening.

"It is time for you to enter state politics," said Blanchard to Thaddeus Stevens, who had been recruited for the statehouse and even Congress by others. To this point, he found little passion in the major parties. He was annoyed with the growing tendency of Democrats to tolerate slavery and realistic about the Federalists or the Whigs' chances of survival. He needed a cause, and Blanchard knew it.

Thaddeus Stevens gave this thought unusually long consideration. He said to Reverend Blanchard: "It is time. We are through living in the meantime." ✷

CHAPTER EIGHT

June 1831

The Antimasons gathered in Hagerstown, Maryland to hear Thaddeus Stevens open his campaign against Masonry:

> The meeting was addressed by a Mr. Stevens, from your State: a stout man, about 40 years of age, with a bald head, and lame . . . Of his speech, it is enough to say that it was a compound of the vilest slanders, barefaced falsehood, and pandemoniac malignity, that ever fell from the lips of any man . . . (from the Compiler 6/31 in Current, 1942, p. 17)

Stevens may not have impressed his southern audience, and he certainly wasn't surprised to see his archenemy, Jacob LeFever, publish the account. He was taken aback by the physical description and would, from that day forward, wear a reddish-brown wig to cover the baldness that was the result of his bout with "brain-fever" several years before. But the battle with the Masons was engaged.

The Antimasonic party met again in Baltimore in September of 1831, and Stevens shared a hotel room with William H. Seward. They agreed to join forces in support of William Wirt for President, and both found themselves actively involved in national politics against the formidable

Henry Clay and Andrew Jackson. This feisty performance set the stage for his first run for the Pennsylvania House of Representatives in 1833.

The new "gentleman from Gettysburg" was hardly new or gentle. While dabbling with the mundane issues that confronted the General Assembly, he reserved his best fury for the drama that was playing out on another stage. He railed against "King Jackson" and Clay, whom he thought manipulative and insincere (Current, 1942, p. 20). Still, he maintained a connection with Clay's Whigs as he pummeled Jackson, Masons, and Governor Wolf whom, Stevens asserted, abused the Pardons process to free "brethren of the mystic tie."

Stevens wasted no time in establishing himself as an orator with a biting edge to his words. In his first term, he saw opportunities even when the legislature was discussing mundane topics.

In March 1834, the issue was a motion to publish a report from the House Ways and Means Committee. Stevens supported the motion but managed to turn his remarks toward bigger targets: Governor Wolf and President Jackson:

> It is true Pennsylvania is a great and powerful state. Great in the extent of her territory, in the fertility of her soil; in the riches of her minerals; and in the industry of her inhabitants . . . But it makes the soul of the patriot die within him to see the heart's blood of this great state, sucked by the creeping vampyres, and her bones crushed by the Hyenas and Jackals of party! . . . Expose as you will the evils, the errors, the faults and dangerous usurpations of Andrew Jackson, and the satraps of power immediately surround them with the glory of the Eight of January. The victory of New Orleans so dazzles the eyes of freemen that they can scrutinize no further . . . Heaven grant that victory may not prove to be the ruin of our country! (Palmer, Vol. 1, 1997, pp. 12, 16)

Thaddeus Stevens and Public Education

Pennsylvania's commitment to public education goes back to 1824 when a law called for establishing schools in which all children should be admitted and taught without regard to social or financial status. That law was voluntary, and few localities could afford that investment on their own.

It was not until Governor George Wolf, a progressive Democrat, called for a state-funded school system that things began to happen. In the 1833–34 legislative session, a joint committee explored the subject and passed the Free School Act with strong bipartisan support.

It was not long before citizens discovered that providing education for all would not be easy or cheap. The threat of new taxes caused a mutiny in the very next session. The House was flooded with petitions asking for a repeal of the law, and Free Schools seemed doomed.

It was in this atmosphere that Thaddeus Stevens, now in his second term as a member of the Pennsylvania House of Representatives, rose to give his famous "Free Schools Speech" on April 11, 1835.

Excerpts of the Free Schools Speech:

> If an elective republic is to endure for any great length of time, every elector must have sufficient information, not only to accumulate wealth and take care of his pecuniary concerns, but to direct wisely the Legislature, the Ambassadors, and the Executive of the nation . . . If, then, the permanency of our government depends upon such knowledge, it is the duty of government to see that the means of information be diffused to every citizen.

> . . . It is no uncommon occurrence to see the poor man's son, thus encouraged by wise legislation, far outstrip and bear off the laurels from the less industrious heirs of wealth. Some of the ablest men of the present and past days never could have been educated except for that benevolent system. Not to mention any of the living, it is well known that the architect of an immortal name [Benjamin Franklin], who "plucked the lightnings from heaven, and the scepter from tyrants," was the child of free schools .

> . . . And so cast our votes that the blessing of education shall be conferred on every son of Pennsylvania; shall be carried home to the

poorest inhabitant of your mountains so that even he may be prepared to act well his part in this land of freemen . . . so that he may be prepared to . . .lay on earth a . . .solid foundation for that enduring knowledge which goes on increasing through . . . eternity.

On the strength of his arguments, the legislature abruptly halted the repeal effort and, in fact, increased funding for the public-school experiment. Pennsylvania took its place as the leader in education and went on the enshrine the principle of a "thorough and efficient education" for all children in its Constitution.

Stevens himself would state later that defending free schools for all children was his finest legislative accomplishment.

There were other state matters to tend to as well. Stevens applied his prodigious work ethic to addressing those issues. His early legislative forays included efforts to bolster the manufacturing base of the state, support the western expansion of the Commonwealth, support education funding at all levels—including a foundational appropriation of $18,000 for the newly established Pennsylvania College, while he continued to badger the Freemasons with restrictions on their participation on juries and other civic limitations.

His depth of knowledge and oratorical skills served him well. His outspokenness, however, soon drew hostility, and he drew an opponent in his first reelection bid. Thaddeus Stevens set out to eviscerate one Mr. James Cooper, Jr.

Boldly, young Thaddeus Stevens ignored most of the rules of political engagement. He invited himself to Cooper's meetings and commandeered the floor of many taverns and community rooms to rebut the candidate. He managed to have an election day letter printed in the *Star and Banner* newspaper (in which he had a financial interest). The letter pulled no punches:

To James Cooper, Esq.—Your ravings are those of a madman, not those of an accountable human being . . . Do you think that anyone will credit such a charge against a high-minded, honorable man like

Mr. Stevens, on the testimony of an ungrateful apostate, dishonored wretch like you? (Hoch, 2005, p. 78)

James Cooper was an early victim of the wrath of Thaddeus Stevens. He was defeated handily.

Stevens turned his attention to the Governor's race in 1835. Even though he supported and championed Democrat George Wolf's platform of universal free schools, he could not pass up the opportunity to exploit the unease that it caused among taxpayers.

There still was some life in the Anti-Mason movement in Pennsylvania due largely to the continuing war of words between Thaddeus Stevens and pro-Mason editors in the Gettysburg area. Stevens, Amos Ellmaker, Thomas Burrowes, Theophilus Fenn, and Harmer Denny, among others, had turned their own biases and the murder of anti-Mason editor William Morgan in New York into a cause. Pennsylvania was ripe for Anti-Masonry. The notion of a secret society reverberated with groups like the Pennsylvania Germans and the plain sects who opposed the taking of oaths and found many of the intimations about early Masonry to be distasteful.

In addition to their Anti-Mason focus, the Stevens faction expanded their attack on Governor George Wolf. They pointed out extravagance and corruption and railed against the new taxes imposed by the Wolf administration.

By 1835, the Anti-Masons found themselves helped enormously by a wave of opposition to the new "common schools" program espoused by Wolf and passed overwhelmingly by the legislature. Stevens was among the strongest proponents of the public education experiment, but he was not above exploiting the overwhelming opposition to the new taxes in a political fight. At the State Jackson Democrat convention of 1835, Governor Wolf was denied re-nomination. Instead, the frugal Pennsylvania Dutch and Germans united around Henry Muhlenberg of Reading. During the convention, a deadlock occurred, predictably and colorfully, between the "Wolves" and the "Mules." Enough splinter groups stayed with Wolf to destroy Muhlenberg in November. Ritner, in his third standard-bearing role for the Anti-Masons, won the Governorship: Ritner: 94,023, Wolf: 65,804, Muhlenberg, 40,586.

Stevens and the Anti-Masons ran Joseph Ritner for Governor and contested for dozens of seats in the General Assembly. Ritner, having lost twice previously, rode to victory on the strength of Anti-Mason rhetoric and the split among the Democrats.

With an ally in the Governor's office and newly elected Anti-Masons surrounding him, Stevens accelerated his attacks on Freemasonry.

The overwhelming, enduring passion of Thaddeus Stevens, though, was the abolition of slavery. Stevens was unabashed about thrusting his cause in front of an audience that he could whether it was on the campaign trail or in the halls of the legislature.

The Anti-Masonic party was still in its infancy, but Thaddeus Stevens was intent on bringing the entire movement along with him on his abolitionist quest. At their annual convention he rose to offer the following resolution:

> Resolved, that all men are created equally free and that they are endowed by their Creator with certain inalienable rights, among which are life, liberty, and the pursuit of happiness.
>
> Resolved, That it is the duty of a Republican Government to protect every human being in all his inalienable rights, so far as it can be done without violating the fundamental laws of the government.
>
> Resolved, That Congress possesses the constitutional right to abolish Slavery and the Slave-trade, in the District of Columbia, and the territories of the United States . . .
>
> Resolved, That Congress possesses power to prohibit the admission of any State into the Union, which tolerates Slavery by its Constitution; and that it is their duty to enforce such prohibition."
>
> (Palmer, 1997, pp. 50, 51)

Stevens had also found a new target for his political passions—Philadelphia. At public gatherings and on the House floor, Stevens railed

against "the overgrown influence of the city and county of Philadelphia."
He alleged fraud in the city's census and antagonized leaders alike by
suggesting that Jefferson himself had said: "great cities were great sores
on the body politic." (Hoch, 2005, p. 112)

It wasn't long before Philadelphia would have its revenge.

CHAPTER NINE

December 1837

When the forty-eighth session of the General Assembly began in Harrisburg on December 5, 1837, Stevens reassumed his position as the chief inquisitor and self-appointed conscience of that body. His attacks on Philadelphia and his ruthless style in debates generated resentment among some of his colleagues.

While most Pennsylvania leaders were focused on recovering from the recession caused by the Panic of 1837, Stevens continued to pursue his agenda. This included trial by jury rights for fugitive slaves (which passed the House but died in the Senate), and a land transaction that brought two townships in Franklin County into his own Adams County area. It was no coincidence that the land housed the Caledonia Iron Works, which was owned by Stevens.

Stevens aroused additional suspicion when, in partnership with the Ritner administration, he helped shape the extension of the Pennsylvania Railroad through the central part of the state. Some of the twists and turns in the track were suspected to bring freight closer to Stevens' manufacturing facilities, and it was dubbed "Stevens' Tapeworm." This imagery began to appear in editorials and political pamphlets.

Joseph Ritner, at Steven's urging, became the first Governor to condemn slavery. The white electorate of Pennsylvania did not look fondly on his stance, and he was dubbed "His Black Majesty" by some. Those types of epithets rolled off Stevens' back, but Ritner paid the political price.

Stevens returned to the House in 1838, but Joseph Ritner was defeated by a Jackson/Buchanan Democrat by the name of David Porter. The Democrats were resurgent, but a violent power struggle was soon to engulf the state capitol.

The seeds of the Buckshot War were sown in October 1836 at a convention convened by the legislature to consider reforms. Thaddeus Stevens, to the astonishment of Anti-Mason and Whig leaders, had lost his reelection bid to the statehouse that year. By a handful of votes, the people of Adams County had rejected Stevens' outspoken style. They had grown concerned about his pronouncements on race and the school tax, and they sent a neophyte to Harrisburg in his place.

Still, Stevens managed to get himself appointed as a delegate to the convention, and quickly split the proceedings apart with vituperative remarks borne of his recent defeat. One colleague noted that Stevens had become the "great unchained" as he put forth resolutions on everything from public education to anti-Jackson screeds to voting rights for African Americans.

On this last issue, a former ally named William Meredith became an enemy: "I know no good reason why they (the Negroes) should be admitted to the political class." (Hoch, 2005, p. 117).

The suffrage vote collapsed and infuriated Stevens. This defeat and the lingering sting of his temporary ousting from the legislature engendered even stouter advocacy in him. He made sure that his electoral bases were covered and won the elections in 1837 and 1838. His focus remained on slaves, education, and small communities. His brash pronouncements and legislative forays—including his adventures into Philadelphia politics—set the stage for insurrection.

The election of 1838 was fraught with charges of voter fraud and official manipulation. The Jackson Democrats flexed control of the big City machinery, but the Anti-Masons and Whigs felt they had their strongholds that would carry the day.

Stevens masterminded what he thought was a win for his coalition members, but he could not carry Ritner to reelection. Thus, as a lame duck, the Governor had limited powers to assist his allies as they tried to reorganize the House and Senate.

Upon arrival in Harrisburg, candidates found that two completely different sets of election returns had been presented to the Secretary of the Commonwealth. Secretary Thomas H. Burrowes, a Whig sympathizer, huddled with Thaddeus Stevens to address the situation. They settled on a loophole in Pennsylvania law relating to how election returns were to be conveyed to the state. Accordingly, many of the votes from Philadelphia were discounted, and the Stevens faction claimed control in both the House and Senate.

Stevens and Burrowes became the target of Democrats who vowed to overturn their political treachery—by force, if necessary.

Forty Stevens cronies met at Wilson's Hotel to plan to install a T.S. Cunningham as Speaker of the House. The Philadelphia faction was planning its activities.

> As members of Pennsylvania's House of Representatives assembled in the Capitol on the morning of Tuesday, December 4, 1838, they found the lobby, gallery, and floor of the House crowded with dangerous, suspicious-looking men. Stevens said he had difficulty entering the House and getting to his chair because of the mob. (Hoch, 2005, p. 134)

Stevens would later write that "My seat had the honor of being guarded by eight or ten men of the most desperate brawlers of Kensington and Spring Garden, who thrust themselves determinedly against my chair . . . they were armed with double-barreled pistols, bowie knives, and dirks." (Hoch, 2005, p. 135)

In fact, John J. McCahen, a Postal official from Philadelphia, served as the leader of the armed insurgents, and all eyes were on him to give them the signal.

Stevens ignored the dangers and rose to conduct business his way.

"Mr. Speaker," he shouted, "I ask that the Chair recognize the election of Thomas S. Cunningham as the rightfully elected Speaker of the House."

Cunningham took the podium from the interim Speaker, a Bible was produced, the oath was administered, and the House was immediately gaveled into recess.

McCahen stood defiantly at the Speaker's podium and whispered to Cunningham: "And you shall never meet in this House again." (Hoch, 2005, p. 136)

For their part, the Philadelphia Democrats nominated William Hopkins, swore him in, and adjourned.

Similar chaos existed at the reorganization of the Senate. Sen. Charles B. Penrose presided, but, once again, the election returns presented by Secretary of the Commonwealth Burrowes were met with uproar. Stevens, observing from the cloakroom, wrote:

"The people in the gallery raised the most hideous uproar; shouting, threatening violence to Penrose, Burrowes, and Stevens, and finally broke over the railing and rushed with great noise into the Senate chamber. There seemed to be hundreds of voices at the same time demanding vengeance, mobbing, riding on a rail, and demanding death to Burrowes, Penrose, and myself."

———

In a madcap moment of legislative history, Burrowes and Penrose retreated to the cloakroom and encountered Stevens. "What shall we do?" asked an agitated Burrowes.

Stevens, cooler under pressure than most, assessed the situation and took control:

"Jump!" he said.

And the three proceeded to exit via a window that was six or eight feet above ground level. One observer noted that Burrowes lagged behind as Stevens and Penrose jogged toward the river to wait out the daylight among the bushes.

"Help!" cried Burrowes, "they've got me!" He was sure that one of the Philadelphia thugs was holding on to his long black coat.

"You damned coot," said Stevens, "you're snagged in a thorn bush!"

At nightfall, the three made their way to the Governor's residence and safety. ✳

———

Governor Ritner issued a plea to law enforcement to secure order and called up the First Division of Pennsylvania's National Guard from Philadelphia. The commander of the division was not enthusiastic about quelling what he saw as a political dispute—and one that was anti-Philadelphia at that. He ordered troops to carry buckshot as ammunition and would spend the next three weeks keeping a careful watch on as many as 400 armed insurgents in Harrisburg.

The tension came to a head when State Senator Jacob Cassatt, a Stevens/Penrose/Cunningham ally, took to the floor to make one last attempt to recognize the "Cunningham House" over the "Hopkins House." He took his stand on Christmas day.

He was found dead in his hotel room the next morning. While no foul play was proven, speculation was that intimidation by the mob was the cause of death—and that Thaddeus Stevens was next.

That day, Stevens took pen in hand and resigned via a letter to his constituents: "The liberty of ourselves and of your posterity can be preserved only by refusing to yield anything to lawless rebellion . . . Preferring retirement to dishonor, I withdraw from the Legislature." (Hoch, 2005, p. 147)

Several counties held new elections in January and, with a new Governor, Whigs and Anti-Masons began to return to their seats—grudgingly recognizing the Hopkins House. All returned but Thaddeus Stevens, who remained on his principled sabbatical.

The new leadership attempted to address the matter by declaring the Stevens seat open. A new election was held, and Stevens was duly elected and sworn in with six days left in the session.

Thaddeus Stevens would serve two more terms in the Pennsylvania House of Representatives but found little satisfaction in being a back-bencher. He would leave the legislature and the Gettysburg area for good in 1843.

Stevens made sure that he was accepted by the County bar and settled into his new home and law office on Queen Street in Lancaster, Pennsylvania.

While he would tend to business and his law practice for five years, he found time to support Presidential candidates and to keep his contacts warm for reentry into politics at the right time and the next level.

CHAPTER TEN

Lydia Hamilton Smith

Lydia Hamilton Smith had been a part of Thaddeus Stevens' life since their first encounter in Harrisburg in 1838. Upon the death of her husband, the carpenter Isaac Smith, Lydia sought out Stevens and was promptly retained as his housekeeper in 1848. He was 56. She was 35. From the start of their arrangement, Stevens was protective of "Mrs. Smith." She was the undisputed mistress of the household. She was not demanding in the least, but Stevens made sure that courtesies were extended to her to the extent that townsfolk soon began calling her not "Mrs. Smith" but "Mrs. Stevens."

At the end of his life, Thaddeus Stevens would stir up a controversy that would be eternal by selecting a gravesite to accommodate himself and his Lydia. Here is what the Lancaster Intelligencer wrote about It on July 6, 1867:

> Nobody doubts that Thaddeus Stevens has always been in favor of negro equality, and here, where his domestic arrangements are so well known, his practical recognition of his pet theory is perfectly well understood . . . There are few men who have not given to the world such open and notorious evidence of a belief in negro equality as Thaddeus Stevens. A personage, not of his race, a female of dusky hue, daily walks the streets of Lancaster when Mr. Stevens is

at home. She has presided over his house for years. Even by his own party friends, she is constantly spoken of as Mrs. Stevens, though we fancy that no rite of Mother Church ever gave her a right to it. It is natural for men to desire to sleep their last with those they loved in life. If Thaddeus Stevens insists on being buried side by side with the woman he is supposed to have taken to his bosom, it is entirely a matter of taste. But why did he not purchase a lot in an African bury-ing ground at once? There no white man's bones would have jostled his own, and she who has so long been his most intimate associate might have been gathered to his side without exciting public scandal. (Brodie, 1959, pp. 91, 92)

Even his good friend, Jonathan Blanchard, one of the very few who would risk the wrath of the Old Commoner, wrote to Stevens in 1865: "At present in every part of the United States, people believe that your personal life has been one prolonged sin; that your lips have been defiled with blasphemy, your hands with gambling, and your body with women . . . Now you owe it to yourself and your mother's God, to leave some means of correcting this belief, if false, or to show that you have always condemned and despised yourself on account of these besetting sins! . . . The good you have done the country (and none have done more, if so much) is no offset for vices such as I have named above."

The recorded response from Stevens was surprisingly meek and tell-ing. "Probably as between our Creator and us, all of us are somewhat deficient. I know I am deplorably so. But as to my fellowmen, I hope so to live that no one shall ever be wronged or suffer on my account." (Korngold, pp. 11, 12)

Southern editors, who had swallowed a bellyful of Stevens harsh rhetoric and unceasing abolitionist fervor, before, during and after the war, took much harsher shots looking for one final arrow that could pierce the heart of their aging nemesis. This from an Alabama paper in 1867:

In the city of Lancaster, nigh upon the pure city of Philadelphia, Thaddeus Stevens has for years lived in open adultery with a mulatto

woman, whom he seduced from her husband, a full-blooded
negro . . . I only mention the fact that the ultra-super sanctimonious
saints of the African Ascendancy may get the beam out of their own
eyes before they gouge mercilessly at the motes of others. (Korngold,
1955, p. 74)

The only real response to any of these attacks came when Stevens
took pen to paper in a letter to Mr. W. B. Mellins. In the almost illegible
scrawl of the palsied hand of old age, he wrote:

In the course of my life, I have received a very large number of such
attacks. Perhaps no man in the state has received more slanders or
been charged with more vices or malignant crimes than I have . . . As
to the domestic history, I have only to say, that the whole is totally
without foundation, except so far as follows: From the time I began
business (forty-odd years ago) I have kept house, through the agency
of hired servants, having no female relations. Those servants were
of various colors, some white, some black, others of intermediate
colors. My inquiry was only into their honesty and capacity. They
have resided with me for various periods, from one month to fifteen
years, generally more than one at a time . . . I believe I can say that no
child was ever raised, or, so far as I know, begotten under my roof . . .
(Korngold, 1955, p. 76)

The biographers, Brodie, Singmaster, Korngold, and even Current
tread gingerly around the 20-year relationship between Thaddeus Stevens
and Lydia Hamilton Smith. Stevens, however, does not, in any way, deny
the suggestion of intimacy.

Beverly Palmer, who did brilliant work chronicling the Stevens'
Papers, had this to say:

Many have speculated as to whether Stevens' mulatto housekeeper,
Lydia Hamilton Smith, as his mistress. Smith came to work for him
in 1848, and remained in his household, regularly traveling back

and forth with him from Lancaster to Washington, until his death. Certainly, she was a good friend to his nephews and other family members, because their letters to Stevens contain frequent warm and cordial references to her. Characteristically, his one surviving letter to Mrs. Smith reveals little, except that he did not treat her like a servant, but (at the least) as a highly regarded friend. (Palmer, 1997, p. 176)

Perhaps the most overt comments on the Stevens/Smith relationship come from Bradley Hoch in "Thaddeus Stevens in Gettysburg." On Smith: "Over the years she became more than just his employee. Stevens had finally found the woman who became the love of his life." (Hoch, 2005, p. 245)

The only surviving correspondence to Lydia from Thaddeus came amid the Civil War:

To Lydia Hamilton Smith
Washington, July 24, 1861
Mrs. Lydia Smith

Dear Madam:
I am glad to hear that you are well—I am no worse than usual—We have had a bloody battle and a bad defeat—But men are not discouraged
I think Congress will adjourn next week and I shall be home the week after—Thaddeus and Alanson were not in the battle; I suppose they will soon go home—Give my respects to Mrs. Erle and all the friends

Yours, Thaddeus Stevens

CHAPTER ELEVEN

March 1848

Stevens completed his service in the Pennsylvania legislature and set his sights on new adventures. Gettysburg had become a bit too confining, and the Legislature proved to be too small a forum for his world view. He moved to the larger City of Lancaster and grew his various businesses and his law practice.

His appetite for public discourse never abated. It was during this brief "civilian" period that he struck up correspondence and alliances with figures about to burst on the political scene.

Seward and Simon Cameron from Pennsylvania, Salmon Chase, and Samuel Galloway from Ohio, John Sergeant of Massachusetts, John McLintock of the newly constituted Pennsylvania (Gettysburg) College, and John Jay, Chief Justice of the US Supreme Court, communicated with him.

In a precursor to the maelstrom in which he was about to enter, Stevens received this note from an ambitious politician from Springfield, Illinois:

September 3, 1848
Hon: Thaddeus Stevens
Dear Sir:
You may possibly remember seeing me at the Philadelphia
Convention—introduced to you as the lone Whig star of

Illinois—Since the adjournment, I have remained here, so long in the Whig document room—I am now about to start for home; and I desire the undisguised opinion of some experienced person and sagacious Pennsylvania politician, as to how the vote of that state, for governor, and president is likely to go—In casting about for such a man, I have settled upon you; and I shall be much obliged if you will write me at Springfield, Illinois.

The news we are receiving here now, by letters from all quarters is steadily on the rise; we have none lately of a discouraging character— This is the sum, without giving particulars—Yours truly, A Lincoln

Lincoln's immediate interest was the Presidential bid of Zachary Taylor, but Stevens' response in his typically candid tone, assessed that race and a possible Lincoln candidacy in the future: "I have some, but not strong hopes of Penna. If the Phila. Whigs had common sense, we could carry the state . . . I fear we cannot count on either Indiana or Ohio . . . (Palmer, 1997, pp. 102, 103)

CHAPTER TWELVE

October 1850

In Congress, October 1850, Stevens had stirred up controversy with his stance on the Christiana Riots and was increasingly disenchanted with the major parties and their leaders at the national level. There was also another reason that he was brooding about public service at this moment.

In a letter to his friend and partner, John McPherson, Stevens noted the difficulty of maintaining a business and holding Congressional leadership positions simultaneously:

> October 13, 1850
> Dear sir:
> . . . I have been greatly disappointed at the operations of my iron-
> works this season. Bad as the times are I had expected them to realize
> at least $5,000, and still think they should have done it—Instead
> of that I have paid out of my own funds several thousand to keep
> them going—This, and my foolish absence in Congress have greatly
> deranged my calculations—
> I have come to the determination to (use) up the stock on hand, and
> such further amount is necessary to work the present to advantage,
> and close operations, sell off all the property real and personal to pay
> off my debts—

This will all be done in the next twelve months—If there should be any deficiency, I shall resign my seat in Congress, and devote my time to paying the balance, and making a living . . .
Thaddeus Stevens

PART THREE

THE FIRE

CHAPTER THIRTEEN

October 1859

Some say the earth will end in fire,
Some say in ice.
From what I've tasted of desire
I hold with those who favor fire.
But if it had to perish twice,
I think I know enough of hate
To say that for destruction ice
Is also great
And would suffice.
("Fire and Ice," Robert Frost in the Oxford Book of American Verse,
    1973, p. 567)

Harper's Ferry rests where the Shenandoah and Potomac rivers come together, about sixty miles from the nation's capital. Because the climate and terrain precluded extensive tobacco or cotton cultivation, there were no large plantations in the region. The population of the entire six-county surrounding area included 115,000 whites, almost 10,000 freed Negroes, and only 18,000 slaves, many of whom were women and children.

After his final conversations with his supporters in Boston, Brown set about rounding up the recruits—mostly fugitive slaves residing in Canada—whom he expected would join his volunteer army. He then set out for the Harper's Ferry region and from his station at the Kennedy farmhouse, wrote letters to John, Jr. instructing him to send on the volunteers. Hardly any came. In late September, the 950 pikes, which he had purchased from Charles Blair of Connecticut, arrived, and in the next two weeks, a few late recruits joined the party. Although John Kagi's draft plan for The Provisional Army called for a brigade of over 4,500men (divided into four regiments, sixteen battalions, and sixty-four companies), Brown started with only twenty-one followers (sixteen whites and five blacks), less than a third of a company. He intended to add liberated slaves to his volunteer army until it achieved brigade level; organizationally, if, in no other way, Brown was prepared for success.

Finally, Brown decided to strike. At eight o'clock Sunday night, October 16, he left for Harper's Ferry with eighteen of his men, leaving three behind to move the supplies to another location where they could arm the slaves and others who would surely join the fight. Brown's band met no resistance entering the town and quickly secured the United States armory and arsenal and seized a rifle works. Brown next sent out some of his men to round up hostages from nearby farms and to spread the news to the slaves that their liberation was at hand. A while later, Brown's men stopped a Baltimore-bound train entering Harper's Ferry, only to let it pass through and allow the trainmen to alert others to what was going on. By Monday morning Harper's Ferry was filled, not with slaves come to join the insurrection, but with armed farmers and angry militiamen come to suppress it.

This is how Warch describes the beginning of the insurrection (Warch, 1973, pp. 59–60).

His small band of abolitionists would be routed, and John Brown would be hung. For years, his actions would be debated in the public press and fora throughout north and south. He had traveled throughout the country pursuing one business scheme after another and had proven time and time again that he was relentless. Even when it meant yearlong separations from his wife and children, Brown was dedicated to whatever vision was at hand.

His early military experience had been undistinguished, but he was a voracious reader and an aficionado of military strategies and organization. His desperate, lifelong struggle for success and his deep religious convictions converged on the matter off slavery. He alone could plan for years and write passionately to patrons for support for the upcoming quest. He alone could suffer the forced march to Harper's Ferry with the reassurance that his cause was just, and his message would resound among the oppressed.

George Bernard Shaw would write later that: "The reasonable man adapts himself to the world; the unreasonable one persists in trying to adapt the world to himself. Therefore, all progress depends on the unreasonable man."

Southerners viewed Brown as diabolical, radical, and insane.

Northerners, abolitionists included, had similar views. Slaves in the Harper's Ferry area were perplexed; not inspired. The entire enterprise was condemned for its fanatical application of force even against the evil of slavery.

Lincoln himself, who would build a national campaign against the injustice of slavery, treated the incident gingerly and distanced himself and his fledgling party from the deeds.

> John Brown was no Republican, and you have failed to implicate a
> single Republican in his Harper's Ferry enterprise . . . John Brown's
> effort was peculiar. It was not a slave insurrection. It was an attempt
> by white men to get up a revolt among slaves, in which the slaves
> refused to participate. In fact, it was so absurd that the slaves, with all
> their ignorance, saw plainly enough it could not succeed. That affair,
> in its philosophy, corresponds with many attempts, related in history,
> as the assassination of kings and emperors. An enthusiast broods
> over the oppression of a people till he fancies himself commissioned

by Heaven to liberate them. He ventures the attempt, which ends in little else than his own execution . . . (Cooper Union Address 2/27/60, pp. 132, 133)

But the commitment and demeanor of John Brown during and following the incident raised Harper's Ferry to a defining historical event. He was determined to free slaves; not to kill federal troops. He passed up numerous opportunities to murder, intent instead on proclaiming his message. This eyewitness account from a captured clerk, a man by the name of John E. P. Daingerfield, sees more method than madness:

> . . . All the stores, as well as the arsenal, were in the hands of Brown's men, and it was impossible to get either arms or ammunition, there being hardly any private weapons. At last, however, a few arms were obtained, and a body of citizens crossed the river and advanced from the Maryland side. They made a vigorous attack, and in a few minutes, caused all the invaders who were not killed to retreat to Brown inside of the armory gate . . . Then commenced a terrible firing from without, at every point from which the windows could be seen, and in a few minutes, every window was shattered, and hundreds of balls came through the doors . . . This was kept up most of the day . . .
>
> . . . During the day and night, I talked much with Brown. I found him as brave as a man could be, and sensible upon all subjects except slavery. He believed it was his duty to free the slaves, even if, in doing so, he lost his own life. During a sharp fight, one of Brown's sons was killed . . . Brown did not leave his post at the porthole; but when the fighting was over, he walked to his son's body, straightened out his limbs, took off his trappings, and then, turning to me, said, "This is the third son I have lost in this cause."

John Brown's cause was met with furious reprisal when a young Colonel by the name of Robert E. Lee arrived with government troops and sent J.E.B. Stuart with a flag of truce to Brown to demand surrender. Brown said that he preferred to die there rather than face hanging for insurrection. Stuart told him he had until morning, and no attempt at escape or further provocation was made. When morning arrived, John Brown and his tattered band found themselves hopelessly outnumbered by government troops, local farmers, and militia. This time, there was no option given for surrender as hundreds stormed the armory building. First in was a lieutenant named Green who found Brown and split his skull with the hilt of his sword. The attack continued without mercy until Brown's band was dead or captured.

While Brown bled heavily from head and body wounds, he was interrogated and implicated on the spot not just by government officials but by bystanders. One of them asked: " Upon what principle do you justify your acts?"

Brown replied: "Upon the golden rule. I pity the poor in bondage that have none to help them; that is why I am here . . . You may dispose of me very easily; I am nearly disposed of now, but this question is still to be settled . . ." (Warch, 1973, pp. 73–77)

John Brown's own words upon capture: "My name is John Brown; I have been well known as Old Brown of Kansas. Two of my sons were killed here today, and I'm dying too. I came here to liberate slaves and was to receive no reward. I have aged from a sense of duty . . . I am an old man. Yesterday I could have killed whom I chose, but I had no desire to kill any person and would not have killed a man had they not tried to kill me and my men. I could have sacked and burned the town but did not; I have treated the persons whom I took as hostages kindly, and I appeal to them for the truth of what I say. If I had succeeded in running off the slaves this time, I could have raised twenty times as many men as I have now, for a similar expedition. But I have failed."

Indeed, the imprisoned clerk supported Brown's version: "He had made me a prisoner but had spared my life and that of other gentlemen in his power; and when his sons were shot down beside him, almost any other man would at least have exacted life for life." (Warch, 1973, pp. 62–66)

During his incarceration, the tempest grew, and the storm clouds gathered ominously over north and south. The Rev. Edwin M. Wheelock sermonized that: "John Brown will undoubtedly be hung. 'Tis well. He headed insurrection and became accountable for bloodshed and must be hung. 'Tis well, I repeat . . . There must be a martyr to truth, and each one that falls is a bountiful spring shower upon the buried seed." (Warch, 1973, p. 176)

Even more direct was this lecture from the noted Wendell Phillips: "The Lesson of the Hour?" I think the lesson of the hour is insurrection. Insurrection of thought always precedes the insurrection of arms. The last twenty years have been an insurrection of thought. We seem to be entering a new phase of this great American struggle." (Warch, 1973, p. 43)

A half-century of gloom would soon be emblazoned by the flash of cannon fire. Phillips's "insurrection of thought" was of much longer gestation than twenty years. It had consumed and darkened the age. John Brown lit the fuse.

––––––

The nation faced brutal adolescence in the early 19th century that included constant defense of its own national identity, the perils of expanding frontiers, and the booms and busts of its fledgling economic system. It faced those challenges without the extraordinary genius that marked its birth. The Franklins, Jeffersons, Madisons, and Washingtons were gone or aged, and the next generation was occupied not with aristocratic theories of democratic republicanism but with actually putting the experiment into practice.

To make matters more complicated, life was hard. The generation after the founding fathers, the sons, and daughters of the revolution had to find their way amid the wilds of the woods, in the fields, or at the lathe. They nurtured their system of government not with the refined minds of European educations nor with the condescension of the aristocracy but with the callused hands and lessons learned from the harsh realities of pioneer life.

In his ambitious work about the distinct qualities of each American generation, William Strauss identifies this era as the "Transcendental Generation." Despite the rigors of the frontier, perhaps because of it, a generation of political leaders and writers emerged determined to do more than subsist.

There arose men and women with a sense of destiny, with a purpose rooted in spirituality or similar fervor. Strauss notes: "No generation ever paraded so many visions of godliness—whether Lincoln's Union, Davis' Confederacy, Brigham Young's "Kingdom of Zion," John O'Sullivan's "Manifest Destiny," John Humphrey Noyes' 'perfectionism,' Mary Baker Eddy's Christian Science, Albert Brisbane's utopian communes, Orestes Brownson's Catholic socialism, or Dorothea Dix's severe but redemptive penology." (Strauss, 1991, p. 198)

Alexis de Tocqueville encountered in America "a fanatical and almost wild spiritualism that hardly exists in Europe . . . religious insanity is very common in the United States." Strauss likened the whole period to "a generation of Captain Ahabs, [the] transcendentals from Boston to Charleston turned personal truth into collective redemption." (Strauss, 1991, p. 198)

Among those born to play a role in this zeal:

1792 Thaddeus Stevens
1795 Dred Scott
1797 Sojourner Truth
1800 John Brown
1800 Nat Turner
1801 Brigham Young
1803 William Lloyd Garrison
1807 Robert E. Lee
1807 Henry W. Longfellow
1808 Jefferson Davis
1809 Edgar Allen Poe
1813 John Fremont
1815 Elizabeth Cady Stanton
1817 Frederick Douglass
1817 Henry David Thoreau
1820 Harriet Tubman

THE LIFE AND LOVES OF THADDEUS STEVENS

1820 William Tecumseh Sherman
1820 Susan B. Anthony
1821 Mary Baker Eddy

And some foreign influences:

1795 Thomas Carlyle
1805 Alexis de Tocqueville
1818 Karl Marx
1819 Queen Victoria

To which, there should certainly be added: Abraham Lincoln,
Emerson, Whittier, William Cullen Bryant, Webster, Clay, Calhoun,
Longfellow, Oliver Wendell Holmes, Walt Whitman, Horace Greeley,
James Russell Lowell, and Harriet Beecher Stowe.

The key events of the era:

1831 – Nat Turner's slave rebellion; Garrison launches abolitionism
1848 – "Manifest Destiny" defeats Mexico; Women's Rights
    Convention
1852 – Uncle Tom's Cabin fuels abolitionism in North
1859 – John Brown's raid on U.S. arsenal at Harper's Ferry
1863 – Emancipation Proclamation; Union victorious at Gettysburg
1865 – Lee surrenders at Appomattox; Lincoln assassinated
1868 – Radical Republicans fail to impeach President Johnson
1877 – Reconstruction ends; U.S. troops leave South

The cultural endowment of the era:

The Liberator – William L. Garrison
Walden, Civil Disobedience – Henry David Thoreau
Gettysburg Address – Abraham Lincoln
Encyclopedia Americana – Francis Lieber
Leaves of Grass – Walt Whitman
The Transcendentalist – Ralph Waldo Emerson

The Raven – Edgar Allen Poe
Battle Hymn of the Republic – Julia Ward Howe
The Book of Mormon – Joseph Smith
The Scarlet Letter – Nathaniel Hawthorne
The Rise and Fall of the Confederate Government – Jefferson Davis
(Strauss, 1991, p. 196)

Self-made men and women, not heirs and nobles, mustered the determination to make the country prosper even as they were building their homes with bare hands and educating themselves by candlelight.

These "commoners" not only understood the vision and tenets of William Penn and Alexander Hamilton, but they also put them to the test. What they did not understand was how slavery could continue to exist in the experiment. This curious institution of Southern life became an abomination to some, a necessary evil to others, and, for the transcendental generation, the focus of their most crusading work. It was the backdrop against which social and intellectual dramas unfolded for 75 years.

Again, Strauss puts his finger on the personal furies that whipped the ocean of the 19th century into a frenzy:

> The Transcendentals may have been America's most high-minded generation—but they also became, by any measure, its most destructive. Recalling Robert E. Lee, the younger Henry Adams bitterly remarked after the Civil War was over, "It's always the good men who do the most harm in the world." (Strauss, 1991, p. 199)

> As the young marched off to bloody battle, midlife Transcendentals urged them on with appeals to justice and righteousness. Garrison spoke of the "trump of God," while Phillips warned that the Union was "dependent for success entirely on the religious sentiment of the people." (Strauss, 1991, p. 203)

> Transcendentals transformed into elders, much like those in the novels of Hawthorne and Melville—stern-valued patriarchs, revered but feared (like Thaddeus Stevens) with something supernatural

inhabiting their weary frames . . . They emancipated the slaves, wrote inspiring verse, and preserved the Union their fathers had created. (Strauss, 1991, p. 204)

Harper's Ferry was the flashpoint that ignited the Civil War. The American landscape would be lit with the fire of the zealots for an entire generation while the nation struggled for reconstruction and redemption.

Thaddeus Stevens (April 4, 1792 – August 11, 1868)
(Courtesy of the Library of Congress)

Lydia Hamilton Smith (February 14, 1813 – February 14, 1884)
(Courtesy of the Library of Congress)

Governor George Wolf, Term of Office –
December 15, 1829 to December 15, 1835
(Courtesy of Capitol Preservation Committee and
John Rudy Photography)

Postmaster General Montgomery Blair
(Courtesy of the Library of Congress)

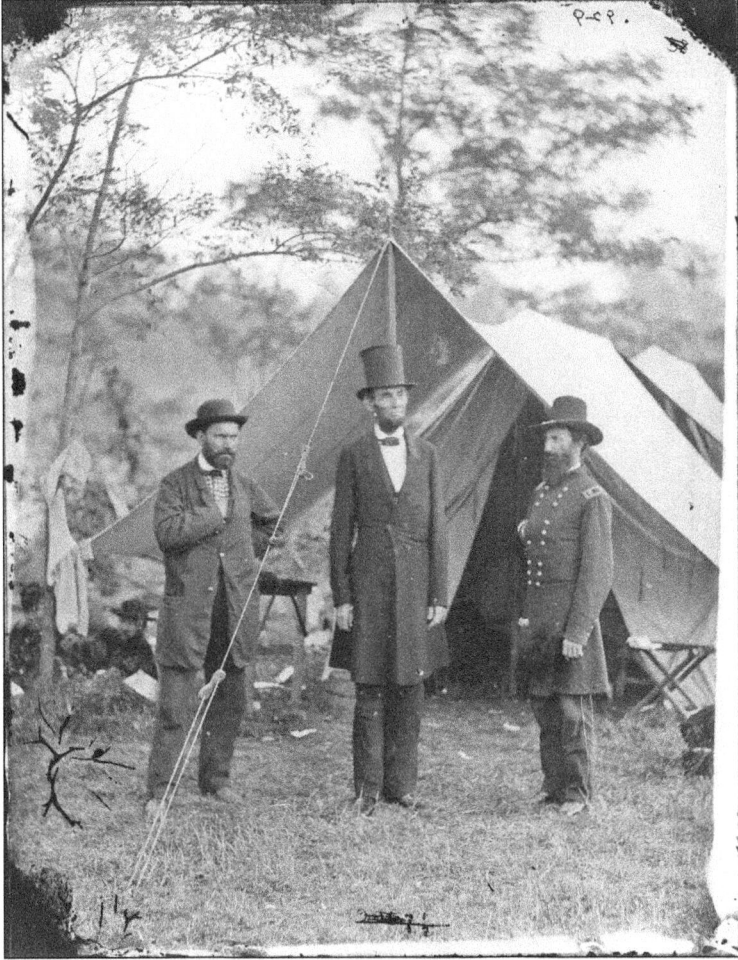

Allen Pinkerton, President Lincoln and General George McLellan at Antietam
(Courtesy of the Library of Congress)

Lincoln's Secretary of War, Simon Cameron
(Courtesy of the Library of Congress)

Stevens (holding a cane) is pictured here with the U.S. House of Representatives' managers of the Johnson impeachment proceedings. (Courtesy of The National Archives/Brady Studios)

President Andrew Johnson's Secretary of War Edwin Stanton
(Courtesy of the Library of Congress)

CHAPTER FOURTEEN

March 1861

The nation's capital, with its granite formality, looked gray and foreboding. Cloudy, rainy days seemed to distort the stark buildings and monuments into monstrous shapes. "A City of mausoleums," thought Abraham Lincoln when he had arrived in the bowels of the Union train station. ✴

Lincoln arrived under the cloak of darkness in the dismal hour of a sullen morning. It was raining on Washington then, and the gloom was appropriate to the nation's mood. The President-elect was inheriting a government that was ripping apart at the seams. Because of the indecision of Buchanan, Fort Sumter had been challenged and would likely be lost. The South Carolina delegation had all but bolted the Congress, and the first southern secession was a virtual certainty. Others would follow unless the new President could buy the time to conciliate. But, Lincoln thought, that's exactly what got his predecessor in trouble.

Lincoln would not have hesitated to reinforce Ft. Sumter. He viewed secession as intolerable—an act of treason—and was prepared to treat it as an Act of War. On the other hand, there was the possibility of staring down the threat. He knew that it would require some gesture. Maybe an olive branch on the slavery question. Perhaps his support for the constitutional amendment would do it.

One thing was certain: more than any inaugural address in history—apart from George Washington's maiden flourish at the helm of the new nation—Abraham Lincoln's address would be scrutinized. Politicians and citizens from north and south would hang on every word for clues as to the very future of the Union. More than a signal, Lincoln knew, it would have to be a strategic work of art.

Lincoln set out immediately to assure the south:

"Apprehension seems to exist among the people of the Southern States that, by the accession of a Republican Administration, their property, and their peace and personal security are to be endangered. There has never been any reasonable cause for such apprehension. Indeed, the amplest evidence to the contrary has all the while existed . . . it is found in nearly all the published speeches of him who now addresses you. I do but quote from one of these speeches when I declare that "I have no purpose, directly or indirectly, to interfere with the institution of Slavery in the States where it exists. I believe I have no right to do so, and I have no inclination to do so."

He went on to quote from his party's platform: ". . . the maintenance inviolate of the rights of the States, and especially the right of each State to order and control its own domestic institutions according to its own judgment, exclusively, is essential . . . and we denounce the lawless invasion by armed force of the soil of any State or Territory, no matter under what pretext as the gravest of crimes."

An extraordinary inaugural gesture was about to become more direct: Lincoln would go on to quote the Constitution upholding the Fugitive Slave law, promise to continue mail delivery, and support a new Constitutional amendment just working its way through the Congress to assure that the Federal Government shall never interfere with the domestic institutions of States, including that of persons held for service. Within three years, the President was to reverse himself on each of these commitments.

As he prepared his inaugural address, Lincoln had only an inkling as to the horrors that lay ahead. He was still recovering from the jarring circumstances of the journey from Springfield. It had been a bone-tiring 12-day trip with the last leg complicated by an assassination plot that was uncovered by Allen Pinkerton. At Pinkerton's suggestion, the official party avoided Baltimore and an unpredictable group of southern saboteurs who reportedly were lying in wait in that City. Instead, the 16th President skulked into Washington under armed guard having spent the night in a rattling car with, of all things, a drunken reveler who insisted on singing "Dixie" most of the way. Northern editors would criticize him severely for the ignominious start to his Presidency, but Lincoln knew the threat was real. It was but the first layer of weight that would be laid directly on his shoulders with unrelenting severity for the rest of his life.

Thaddeus Stevens, the Old Commoner, the Scourge of the South, muttered aloud when Lincoln endorsed the Constitutional Amendment. Stevens had been one of only 65 House members to oppose it, and he was convinced that any conciliation between North and South would be fruitless. Worse, it would provide a false sense of security that would only delay the inevitable and sweep the great moral question of slavery aside once more. The lanky curmudgeon squirmed in his chair on the dais, and President Lincoln's words and tone would set off yet another volley in the Lincoln/Stevens on-again, off-again brawl. ❧

Lincoln's inaugural was but the first declamation of sovereignty that would take place that year. Jefferson Davis stood on the steps of the Capitol in Birmingham several months later and expounded in high-minded fashion on the moral principles that motivated the secessionist movement:

"Our present political position has been achieved in a manner unprecedented in the history of nations. It illustrates the American idea that governments rest on the consent of the governed, and that it is the right of the people to alter or abolish them at will whenever they become destructive of ends for which they were established . . . obstacles may retard, but they cannot long prevent the progress of a movement sanctified by its justice and sustained by a virtuous people."

Then it was Alexander—the other—Stevens' turn. Described by one biographer as "wispy," Stevens, the newly installed Vice President of the Confederacy, was given to coughing attacks and looked frail. His words, however, had the sting of Legree's whip: "Our new government is founded on the opposite idea of the equality of the races . . . Its cornerstone rests upon the truth that the negro is not equal to the white man . . . This government is the first in the history of the world based on this great physical and moral truth."

Into this fierce breach of conflicting passions, the "darkly wise and rudely great " Thaddeus Stevens took the oxymorons of his own emotions into the fray. He interacted with all the prominent figures of the day: Clay, Calhoun, Webster, Greeley, Whittier, Garrison, Cameron, Curtin, Douglas, and, yes, especially Abraham Lincoln.

But this moment was a waterfall for Thaddeus Stevens. He watched as his candidate, the man who led the revolution to establish their new Party, raised his hand to take the oath. Then he cascaded over the watery edge and plummeted with Lincoln's words of conciliation. "He was weak," thought Stevens, "as bad as Buchanan." And he felt his life's work break upon the rocks of political betrayal like a soggy barrel. He should have known; he should have kept his distance and avoided the affiliation with the Republicans. He had learned long ago to set his course and to rely on no one. Thaddeus Stevens brooded mightily on the dais and recalled a passage from Emerson's Self-Reliance. Stevens had made it required reading for all his young law school charges in the Lancaster days:

> What I must do is all that concerns me, not what people think. This
> rule, equally arduous in actual and in intellectual life, may serve
> for the whole distinction between greatness and meanness. It is the
> harder because you will always find those who think they know what

is your duty better than you know it. It is easy in the world to live after the world's opinion; it is easy in solitude to live after our own, but the great man is he who in the midst of the crowd keeps with perfect sweetness the independence of solitude . . . Nothing can bring you peace but yourself. Nothing can bring you peace but the triumph of principles. (Bradley, 1967, pp. 1143, 1149)

The bold party of Lincoln and Stevens had already sunk to a shallowness that sickened Stevens. A hundred years later, Walter Lippman would write: "With exceptions so rare they are regarded as miracles of nature, successful democratic politicians are insecure and intimidated men. They advance politically only as they placate, appease, bribe, seduce, bamboozle, or otherwise manage to manipulate the demanding, threatening elements in their constituencies. The decisive consideration is not whether the proposition is good but whether it is popular—not whether it will work well and prove itself, but whether the active-talking constituents like it immediately." (Kennedy, 1964, pp. 2–3)

Lincoln's first words, in Stevens' view, constituted an immediate retrenchment that belied their great moral cause and the destiny that they had dared to dream together. And in the wretched deep grayness of the day, Stevens felt suddenly, overwhelmingly tired. Maybe the President was right. Maybe union and "secesh" citizens have become accustomed to mediocrity. They are no longer motivated by the rallying cries of great statesmen; they are no longer willing to let those statesmen lead them into hell even for a well-articulated national cause. They want comfort.

He had read de Tocqueville: "If in your view the main object of government is not to achieve the greatest strength or glory for the nation as a whole but to provide for every individual therein the utmost well-being, protecting him as far as possible from all afflictions, then it is good to make conditions equal and to establish a democratic government."

One hundred fifty years later in his follow-up American Journey, Reeves would conclude:

Democracy had done that—brought well-being close—because that was what most of the people wanted most of the time. Democratic politicians might be mediocre, might even be more mediocre than the ones Tocqueville met, but politicians did not make or drive the larger system. The United States, the democracy, was a contract between each individual American and all Americans associated as a government. (Reeves, 1982, pp. 352, 353)

The glory and the frustration of American democracy is that greatness is defined by each American—and that's the way we meant it to be. (Reeves, 1982, p. 357)

If he had a clearer path to the aisle, Stevens would have left the dais. He refused to believe that the nation could rise only to the level of everyone's pettiness. Thoughtless, rabbity people, who, according to D.H. Lawrence, "nibble the face of earth to a desert."

Back in Lancaster, Thaddeus Stevens was, fittingly, alone. He looked into the embers of the fire, and a new thought began to burn. Lincoln was President, but he had abandoned the cause. Lincoln was the Commander-in-Chief, but he was refusing to fight. Who then, would carry on the battle for those in need? Who would hear the cries of the dead Dinah and the thousands like her not yet free? Who would rally for those who had trusted in the union and its principles? Who would stand firm for Lydia and Sarah and young Thad and generations to come?

He knew the answer. It came to him as it always did like a breath of peace on a summer night. A respite in his troubled life that brought meaning and conviction back into focus. His volume of Whittier's recent work was close at hand, and he read this passage:

"A track of moonlight on a quiet lake,
Whose small waves on a silver-sanded shore,

Whisper of peace, and with the low winds make
Such harmonies as keep the woods awake,
And listening all night long for their sweet sake."

Peace crept back into what remained of Thaddeus Stevens' soul. 🦌

———

A seeker of truths in the complex matter of love, Moore writes in his Warrior Wisdom:

> In matters of love, we might be even more romantic than women. The history of the world is studded with tales of man's toil, struggle, and eventual self-sacrifice for love—for a woman, for one's country, for an ideal. We thirst for and express deep love with a daredevil's intensity and an aerialist's agility. Even when our impulses are a bit boyish, even when we take the whole matter too seriously, we have a consuming need for love to flow toward us, and to let our own love flow.
>
> Some men, in great equilibrium and balance, exude a physical glow of compassion and worldly love. Like Zorba the Greek, they love life, wine, their work, old women, dance—everybody, and everything. They are like saints of the sensual. Their bodies seem to swim in love's atmosphere, and anyone who comes near them is affected by its pungent releases. These are men completely in touch with their hearts.
>
> Others feel love in surges. We fall in love and enter a glowing, glorious cosmos, and fall out of love onto the hard asphalt of dreary every day. Sometimes we are drawn to love by the head, sometimes by the heart, sometimes by the sly Don Juan between our thighs . . . To see a man in a state of realized, pure love is to see someone who's simplified everything. If he has a family, his great arms and shoulders surround it with warm protection, and his children go out into the world, transmitting their father's loving confidence. Such a man becomes the giant redwood tree watching at the edge of a glade—a lover like nature itself, nourisher and guard. (Moore, 1993, pp. 117–119)

―――――

Thaddeus Stevens felt like a guardian. If he could not be the lover or the nurturer of the object of his passion, he would be the guardian of the Union and the fortress for precious equality. How tall and strong must he now stand as he anticipated the battles ahead? In that era, with strife and war howling, Stephen Crane had written:

A man said to the universe:

"Sir, I exist!"

"However," replied the universe,

"The fact has not created in me

A sense of obligation." (Crane, 1896, p. 548)

By God, they would take notice, Stevens was thinking, even if the elected ones on the floor of the House and Senate don't get it. Even if they cower like vermin, I will bring them to their responsibilities. "They are ferrets; not falcons," thought Stevens.

―――――

Two days after the inauguration of Abraham Lincoln, Thaddeus Stevens was thinking about what Wordsworth had called "The still, sad music of humanity."

There was much to take in: John Brown, the Confederacy, Lincoln, and the new President's predecessor, James Buchanan—Stevens' constituent and nemesis.

The newly retired president had returned to his estate in Wheatland—two miles from where Stevens now sat—bowed and dismayed. Stevens had no use for his constituent—even if he had risen to the Presidency itself.

The Ann Coleman/James Buchanan story was a favorite of his. He continued to hear that the separation of these betrothed was a matter of miscommunication and that the death of Ann so affected Buck that he entered a prolonged period of public service to occupy himself productively. The alternative would have been to serve dutifully in the burgeoning Coleman Iron Works, thereby avoiding politics and his brush with destiny altogether.

For Stevens, it remained a doubtful premise. A romantic notion, perhaps, but an unlikely soap opera. He so disdained Old Buck that he thought him incapable of any great passion. He had personal experience and allowed his mind to wander to those times that their paths crossed. ✺

―――――

In their first encounter, Buchanan and Stevens collaborated on a trial in York, Pennsylvania, in 1827 where Buchanan was so impressed by the younger man's presentation in the courtroom that he approached him in earnest about joining the Democratic party. Stevens had already served four years on the Gettysburg Borough Council and might have been lured by Buchanan's rising star except for the fact that he had already formed some strong negative opinions about the direction of the Democratic party. Even if Stevens had signed on, it wouldn't have lasted long. The party and the ordinary process of elective office were far too tame for his tastes. Within six years, he would identify a galvanizing movement and lead a party largely of his invention to a formidable presence in the Pennsylvania General Assembly.

By 1835, President Andrew Jackson had recast the Democrat party in his style and according to his crude philosophies. A rugged leader with a celebrated history of heroics against the British and a variety of Indian tribes, Jackson brought his tobacco-spitting, patronage machinery to Washington. The Republican party was not yet even an idea, and other parties were hopelessly factionalized.

While Stevens was focused on state politics, Buchanan was playing on a larger stage. He defeated Stevens' close friend and Anti-Mason schemer, Amos Ellmaker, for a U.S. Senate seat in 1835 and further enraged Stevens with an early pronouncement in that body of his opposition to Congress interfering with slavery in Southern states. Buchanan, thought Stevens, was just another doting Jackson Democrat with their complacent and tolerant view of the continued cancer of slavery.

Stevens, in Buchanan's eyes, was a radical firebrand whose convictions could lead the state and federal governments to ruin. Both viewed each other with disdain. Occasionally though, each had to admit to the other's political prowess. Such was the case when Stevens impressed Buchanan with his legislative in 1835.

To eliminate the possibility of a fractured party in 1837, and to avoid a repeat of the fissure that lost the Pennsylvania Governorship in 1835, Senator Buchanan stepped in. He worked out a deal with President Van Buren. Former Governor Wolf received the fattest plum in Pennsylvania, Collector of the Port of Philadelphia. Muhlenberg became United States Minister to Austria. This cleared the political landscape for a new face, David Porter, who went on to defeat Ritner, and even Stevens marveled at the art of the deal.

The relations between the two eroded steadily over the years, and when Buchanan found himself presiding over a nation that was disintegrating, he found himself besieged on the floor of the U.S. House of Representatives regularly by his Congressman, the gentleman from Lancaster, Thaddeus Stevens.

Stevens was outraged, which was his customary state, by Buchanan's failure to grasp the ominous meaning of the rift between north and south. The President had in fact placed the blame for the tension on "misguided fanatics" who wasted the time of Congress "in violent debates on the subject of slavery" which, in turn, provoked the South to form a party "as fanatical in advocating slavery as were the abolitionists of the North in denouncing it." The President was blaming the opponents of slavery, and specifically, pointing the finger directly at Stevens. (Klein, 1980, p. 104)

Some historians would later side with Buchanan on the issue of miscues that led to the War. Randall would write in the 1930s that a "blundering generation" of politicians and agitators "whipped up" a crisis that culminated in war. (Stampp, 1980, p. 205) Craven was blunter: "The conflict was the work of politicians and pious cranks." But the Republican party had come into being and rallied around its stated disgust for the institution of slavery. Lincoln, Charles Sumner, William Lloyd Garrison, Horace Greeley, Sen. Ben Wade, Rep. Owen Lovejoy, and Rep. Thaddeus Stevens were firmly in the Republican camp and driving a moral agenda toward the horror of war. Benjamin Brown French was among those who knew that the conflict was irrepressible and that Buchanan's timidity was delaying the inevitable. In *A Yankee's Journal,* he wrote:

> Tuesday, January 1 [1861]. I commence this Journal at what still continues to be the seat of Government of "The United States of America," although the sovereign state of South Carolina has Resolved herself out of the Union & will be followed in her suicidal attempt to secede by other states equally foolish. There is at the head of this Government now a weak old man, who fears to exercise the proper functions of President of the United States, and whose course is looked upon as next akin to Treasonable. Would to Heaven that we had another Andrew Jackson there instead of James Buchanan. (French, 1861, p. 338)

Even earlier in the election, Thaddeus Stevens had displayed his usual bluntness on the question of Buchanan's effectiveness: "There is no such person running as James Buchanan. He is dead of lockjaw. Nothing remains but a platform and a bloated mass of political putridity."

So much for Buchanan, Stevens thought. Old Buck would never understand the anger that descended upon him. The former President watched in his last years at an uncomfortably close range as Stevens emerged on the national scene with a vengeance.

———

The causes of the Civil War. When did it start? Who was to blame? Was it irrepressible? Could some other Chief Executive have avoided it? If it was unavoidable, was it worth the cost?"

Hundreds of historians and scholars have already grappled with those exact questions. The clearest, simplest assessment of the debacle that erupted into the Civil War was written against the backdrop of Cold War tensions in the mid-twentieth century by Arthur Schlesinger: "man occasionally works himself into a log-jam [which] must be burst by violence." (Stampp, 1980, p. 213)

The shadow of the Civil War darkened the entire 19th century. Most suggest that the first indicators of irreconcilable differences appeared in the Missouri Compromise of 1820. The charismatic Senator from Kentucky, Henry Clay, rose to prominence with the first of his many famous compromises when he drafted the plan to allow Maine to enter the Union as a Free State and Missouri to enter as a slave state. Designed to mollify the economic and social interests of both North and South, it pleased neither completely and drew into focus their differences. The conciliation and the consternation continued with the same arrangement for Michigan and Arkansas in 1837 and Iowa and Florida in 1846.

In the literary community, the root evil of slavery was justification enough to oppose all compromise. Indeed, the most prominent writers and editors of the day wrote fiery perorations of the South and influenced Northern opinion dramatically. Ralph Waldo Emerson actively opposed slavery; Henry David Thoreau was even more extreme. Thoreau's spirited defense of the perpetrators of the Harper's Ferry incident, "A Plea for John Brown," was viewed by most Republicans as too much. Even Thaddeus Stevens felt that murder in the cause of abolition was unacceptable.

Henry Wadsworth Longfellow and Nathaniel Hawthorne studied together in Massachusetts and formed the bedrock support for such abolition stalwarts as Sen. Charles Sumner.

James Russell Lowell wrote for the *Pennsylvania Freeman* out of Philadelphia, the *National Anti-Slavery Standard*, and for the *London Daily News*. His fictional character Hosea Biglow was a national series in 1848 with his political commentary and opposition to the Mexican War. Lowell and Hosea reemerged in 1862 with caustic wit to bolster the Union cause. President Lincoln and others noted that the comic antics and satire of Hosea Biglow was a more effective weapon in the war than the timid leadership of General McLellan.

As far back as 1831, William Lloyd Garrison began what would be a continuous attack on slavery in *The Liberator* when he wrote:

> I am aware that many object to the severity of my language, but is there not cause for severity? I will be as harsh as truth, as uncompromising as justice on this subject. I do not wish to think, or speak, or

write with moderation. I am in earnest. I will not equivocate. I will not excuse. I will not retreat a single inch, and I WILL BE HEARD.

Walt Whitman recorded the atrocities of the War in his writings, having seen the conflict up close as a medical orderly.

But it was John Greenleaf Whittier who spoke for all the literary voices with his powerful poems. In "Men of the North," he eulogized Robert Rantoul who died at his seat in Congress opposing the Fugitive Slave Law and exhorted the North to take up the cause:

> Men of the North! your weak regret
>   Is wasted here; arise and pay
> To freedom and to him your debt,
>   By following where he led the way!
> (Whittier, 1892, p. 88)

He also staked out the position of Massachusetts in his tirade against the slave trade in Virginia:

> The voice of Massachusetts! Of her free sons and daughters,
> Deep calling unto deep aloud, the sound of many waters!
> Against the burden of that voice, what tyrant power shall stand?
> No fetters in the Bay State! No slave upon her land!
>
> Look to it well, Virginians! In calmness, we have borne,
> In answer to our faith and trust, your insult and your scorn;
> You've spurned our kindest counsels, you've hunted for our lives;
> And shaken round our hearths and homes, your manacles and gyves!
>
> We wage no war, we lift no arm, we fling no torch within
> The fire-damps of the quaking mine beneath your soil of sin;
> We leave ye with your bondmen, to wrestle, while ye can,
> With the strong upward tendencies and god-like soul of man!
>
> But for us and for our children, the vow which we have given
> For freedom and humanity is registered in heaven

No slave-hunt in our borders, no pirate in our strand!
No fetters in the Bay State, no slave upon our land!

In Pennsylvania, James and Lucretia Mott motivated the Quakers to lead the abolitionist cause. Three prominent blacks also emerged with great effect. James Forten was a wealthy sailmaker and patron of THE LIBERATOR. Robert Purveys lived on the Bayberry Estate just outside of Philadelphia and became the president of the American Antislavery Society. William Still led and documented the underground railroad movement. (Klein, 1980, p. 161)

These and other voices grew to a crescendo that influenced political leaders from North and South.

In an odd foreshadowing of the passions that were to pull the union apart, Pennsylvania held its debate on slavery in 1837. On May 2 of that year, a Constitutional Convention convened in Harrisburg to address four specific concerns: 1) the power of the governor, 2) the tenure of judges, 3) the power of the state to regulate banking, and 4) voting for non-whites.

It was this last point that proved to be the finale of the convention, and that escalated into a war of words that was a microcosm and a precursor of what was to follow in the United States Congress.

John Sergeant led the convention through eight months of deliberation and addressed the first three matters with conciliation and compromise. For the most part, the debate was civil and productive. There was a flare-up involving Stevens and a Mr. William H. Meredith of Philadelphia on the constant friction between urban and rural interests. Meredith made the mistake of making an ad hominem attack on Thaddeus. Nothing pleased Stevens more than to counter punch, and he was in rare form that day:

> The extraordinary course of the gentleman from Philadelphia has astonished me . . . I could not imagine on what boiling cauldron he had been sitting to make him foam with all the fury of a wizard who had been concocting poison from bitter herbs . . . The gentleman, among other flattery, has intimated that I have venom without fangs.

Sir, I needed not that gentleman's admonitions to remind me of my weakness. But I hardly need fangs, for I never make offensive personal assaults; however, I may, sometimes, in my own defense, turn my fangless jaws upon my assailants with such grip as I may . . . destitute as I am of the polished manners and city politeness of that gentleman, I have a sufficiently strong native sense of decency not to answer arguments by low, gross, personal abuse . . . I shall fearlessly discharge my duty however low, ungentlemanly and indecent personal abuse may be heaped upon me by malignant wise men or gilded fools. (Hensel, n.d., pp. 10–11)

On the issue of non-whites, with Thaddeus Stevens in the hall, there would be no compromise. Having reserved the right to vote for "white freemen" in Pennsylvania, the convention would be subject to an escalation of rhetoric on the issue of slavery and the concern of the day with possible expansion of the curious institution into new territories.

The convention split between Democrats and the loose coalition of idealists who would become the Lincoln Republican party twenty years later. Stevens didn't need a party affiliation to vent his outrage over the mere thought of human servitude, and he was determined to limit the damage to what the Convention had already done to voting rights. Stevens had spoken out before on this issue as a mere Borough Councilman in Gettysburg ten years earlier, but it was in the convention that he found his new voice against slavery. In a Stevenesque twist, he dominated the last sessions of the convention with an unusual presentation designed to embarrass delegates more than to enlighten them. Entering the Declaration of Independence and the Constitutions of both Pennsylvania and the United States as exhibits, Stevens made the case for abolition with wry wit. The convention was reduced to absurdity, and Pennsylvania's position as a free-soil state was reaffirmed.

For the nation, this was the first eruption of a volcano that would become increasingly violent over the next thirty years. Events occurred on an accelerated basis with a stimulus/response effect that pushed the north and south beyond any reasonable conciliation.

The Wilmot Proviso of 1846 was the handiwork of David Wilmot of Pennsylvania, an ally and mentor of Stevens. The provision enacted by the U.S. Congress sought to prohibit slavery in the territories gained in the Mexican/American War. The measure was a victory for free-soilers but was aimed only at stopping the spread of the cancer. Still, the South was enraged and, most observers knew, it meant that slavery was no longer a Democrat versus Whig issue. It was now a regional debate—north versus south.

As Bernard DeVoto stated in *The Year of Decision, 1846*: "At some time between August and December 1846, the Civil War had begun." The Wilmot Proviso and keen politicos like Stevens had already begun to shape the splintered groups: Barnburners, Wooly Heads, Native Americans, Free Soilers, and Conscience Whigs into a consensus of conscience or at least, into a viable political force that knew an opportunity when it saw it.

Events seemed to cascade fast and furiously after that. It was at that precise moment in history that Thaddeus Stevens took his brand of politics to the national scene as a Congressman from the Lancaster area of Pennsylvania. His local newspaper had seen his fitful rise from country lawyer to local politico to independent businessman and publisher to controversial firebrand in the Pennsylvania State House. The *Lancaster Intelligencer* wrote on August 29, 1848:

> He goes into Congress the predetermined agitator of sectional jealousies and divisions . . . His mission is to be one of Strife, of Division, and of Hatred, and surely there is no one so well qualified to fulfill it. (Brodie, 1959, p. 100)

Eighteen Fifty was a rancorous, wrenching year when the fault line between north and south shifted in seismic proportions. President Zachary Taylor died in office, leaving the redoubtable Millard Fillmore to find his way through the slavery thicket. Southern leaders had become increasingly vocal following the Wilmot Proviso and, led by the fiery John C. Calhoun of South Carolina; they were determined to redress the perceived wrong when it came to deal with the western territories.

For better or worse, the Senate and the House were filled with more contentious talent than at any time before or since. Northern Senators included the wily William Seward of New York, Salmon Chase of Ohio, Lewis Cass of Michigan, Hannibal Hamlin of Maine, and the lion himself, the god-like orator from Massachusetts, Daniel Webster. Horace Mann of Massachusetts won a seat in the U.S. House specifically to engage in the slavery debate. Other Northern House members were Joshua Giddings of Ohio, Andrew Johnson of Tennessee who courageously opposed his own state's slave status, and the darkly wise Thaddeus Stevens from Pennsylvania.

The South was not overmatched. In addition to Calhoun, Jefferson Davis was a strong new voice in the Senate from Mississippi, Stephen Douglas, the "little giant" was from Illinois but weighed in heavily for a compromise that favored southern interests, and Henry Clay from Kentucky who was about to advance another legendary compromise. About Henry Clay, John Randolph of Virginia had said he was "a being, so brilliant yet so corrupt, which, like a rotten mackerel by moonlight, shines and stinks."

Alexander Stevens and Robert Toombs, two House members from Georgia, would enter the fray, and all the players would change history.

It was the Clay Compromise of 1850 that dominated Congress, the newspapers, and the regional resolve throughout that year. Approaching the end of his lifetime of public service, Clay relied heavily on his reputation as a fair and effective arbitrator. He was convincing on the floor of the Senate but even better in his one-on-one dealings with colleagues. It would take all his skills to move a package that contained the following provisions:

- compensation to Texas for territory granted peacefully to New Mexico,
- California was to be admitted to the Union as a free state
- slavery would be abolished in the District of Columbia
- Utah and New Mexico would be admitted and allowed to choose slavery or free state status

- the Fugitive Slave Law would be fortified and enforced with runaway slaves captured in the North considered the property of the South and guaranteed return to their southern owners.

Again, Clay managed to muster support even though the extremists were violently opposed. Southern stalwarts railed against the anti-slavery provision relating to the District of Columbia; Northerners could not abide by the equivocation of Utah and New Mexico—a direct violation of the Wilmot Proviso—nor could they tolerate the language of the Fugitive Slave section.

Years later, in a hospital bed recuperating from back surgery, Sen. John F. Kennedy of Massachusetts, in his book Profiles in Courage, would reflect upon that year and the extraordinary actions of a predecessor, the legendary Daniel Webster. It was clear that Clay needed a champion from the north. It was equally clear that no one was more respected and would be more listened to than Webster. It was also clear, at least to Clay, that the choice was between his compromise and the slippery slope toward secession.

The Seventh of March was the date Webster entered the debate. The power and import of his remarks would emblazon the very date on the minds of historians forever.

Before he delivered his "Seventh of March Address," Webster thought for weeks without sleep about its implications. Writes Kennedy:

> The crowd fell silent as Daniel Webster rose slowly to his feet, all the impressive powers of his extraordinary physical appearance—the great, dark, brooding eyes, the wonderfully bronzed complexion, the majestic domed forehead—commanding the same awe they had commanded for more than thirty years. Garbed in his familiar blue-tailed coat with brass buttons, and a buff waistcoat and breeches, he deliberately paused a moment as he gazed about at the greatest assemblage of Senators ever to gather in that chamber . . . Summoning for the last time that spell-binding oratorical ability, he abandoned his previous opposition to slavery in the territories, abandoned his constituents'

abhorrence of the Fugitive Slave Law, abandoned his own place in the history and hearts of his countrymen and abandoned his last chance for the goal that had eluded him for over twenty years—the Presidency. Daniel Webster preferred to risk his career and his reputation rather than risk the Union.

"Mr. President," he began, "I wish to speak today, not as a Massachusetts man, nor as a Northern man, but as an American and a Member of the Senate of the United States . . . I speak for the preservation of the Union. Hear me for my cause . . . Instead of speaking of the possibility . . . of secession, instead of dwelling in those caverns of darkness . . . let us enjoy the fresh air of liberty and union . . ." (Kennedy, 1964, pp. 63–65)

Southern editors rose to his side, but Webster was universally and permanently damned in the north. Thaddeus Stevens, who witnessed the performance of the fallen angel of the north, said: "I could have cut his damned heart out!" (Brodie, 1959, p. 112)

Again, is was Whittier who captured the agony of the "betrayal":

So fallen! So lost! The light withdrawn
    Which once he wore!
The glory from his gray hairs gone
    Forevermore!
Revile him not, the Tempter hath
    A snare for all;
And pitying tears, not scorn and wrath,
    Befit his fall!
Oh, dumb be passion's stormy rage,
    When he who might
Have lighted up and led his age,
    Falls back in night.
Scorn! would the angels laugh, to mark
    A bright soul driven,

Fiend-goaded, down the endless dark,
    From hope and heaven!
Let not the land once proud of him
    Insult him now,
Nor brand with deeper shame his dim,
    Dishonored brow.
But let its humbled sons, instead,
    From sea to lake,
A long lament, as for the dead,
    In sadness make.
Of all we loved and honored, naught
    Save power remains;
A fallen angel's pride of thought,
    Still strong in chains.
All else is gone; from those great eyes
    The soul is fled:
When faith is lost, when honor dies,
    The man is dead!
Then, pay the reverence of old days
    To his dead fame;
Walk backward, with averted gaze,
    And hide the shame!
(Whittier, 1892, pp. 62–63)

On September 11, 1851, another event occurred within a day's journey of Thaddeus Stevens' home that would test the Fugitive Slave Law
and draw national attention to the menace unleashed.

William Parker was thought to be harboring escaped slaves at his
home in Christiana, Pennsylvania. Edward Gorsuch of Maryland had
come to reclaim his "property" and touched off a riot when negroes
from surrounding farms defended Parker and his family. Gorsuch was
hacked to death by an angry mob of negro women with carving knives.
Dickinson Gorsuch, his son, was saved from the same fate by one of
the fugitive slaves who threw himself on the boy to protect him. The

supposition was that William Still, a black leader in the abolitionist movement, alerted the locals to Gorsuch's arrival, and the riot involved two very prominent names. Frederick Douglass himself offered his home as a refuge for those who fled the scene. Thaddeus Stevens, because of his reputation as a gifted lawyer and an avowed abolitionist was brought on as defense counsel in the succeeding trial.

Stevens successfully defended the participants, but the notoriety reminded his constituents of his volatility. They thought their Congressman to be too fiery a spark near the powder keg of the issues of the day. He lost his House seat in 1852.

The Christiana Riots had more severe implications, however. Both North and South exploited the incident for their political purposes and assured a ratcheting up of the tension that was now irreversible. Stevens agitated from the sidelines while other events pressed against the seams of the Union.

1854 – the Native American Party forms bringing a platform of intolerance for race and religion to federal politics. Members were instructed to declare ignorance when questioned by the press; hence, they were soon called the Know-Nothings. The menacing times proved fodder for their surprising strength despite a warning from Lincoln: "Our progress in degeneracy appears to me to be pretty rapid. As a nation, we began by declaring that "all men are created equal, except negroes." When Know-Nothings get control, it will read " all men are created equal except negroes, and foreigners and Catholics." (Brodie, 1959, p. 121)

1854 – the Kansas-Nebraska Bill, in another concession to the growing political power of the south, allows slavery in new territories

1855 – the fledgling Republican party forms largely in response to the 1854 Act and the growing strength of slave states. Thaddeus Stevens is one of the charter members.

1856 – Sen. Charles Sumner, the patrician abolitionist from Boston, is beaten senseless on the floor of the United States Senate. His assailant, Rep. Preston Brooks from Georgia, "defending the honor of the South," bragged that "I gave him about 30 first-rate stripes . . . towards the last, he bellowed like a calf." Brooks received canes to replace the assault weapon from admirers all over the south, but when he died of a mysterious inflammation of the larynx later that year, a Massachusetts paper wrote that the "fingers of God [had him] about the throat." (Brodie, 1959, p. 125)

1857 – The United States Supreme Court hands down its decision in the Dred Scott case. This would later be reversed by the 14th amendment shepherded through Congress by Thaddeus Stevens. In the meantime, it signaled that no legal resolution of the slave question would be possible.

1858 – Stevens returns to Congress, outraged about Dred Scott and Kansas-Nebraska, with a new coalition of Republicans behind him.

1859 – John Brown and a group of zealots raid Harpers Ferry, murdering in the name of abolition.

1859 – Stevens is involved in at least one exchange on the House floor that leads to knives. Violence would continue throughout the next several years, leading to and during the commencement of the War.

1860 – Abraham Lincoln is elected the 16th President. Crittenden presents one final compromise proposal that is rejected by Congress. Owen Lovejoy brother of slain abolitionist, Elijah Lovejoy is involved in an exchange in Congress:

> LOVEJOY: "There is no place in the universe outside the five points of hell and the Democratic Party where the practice and prevalence of such doctrines would not be a disgrace."
>
> BARKSDALE (MISSISSIPPI): "Order that black-hearted scoundrel and nigger-stealing thief to take his seat or this side of the House will do it!"
>
> LOVEJOY: "Nobody can intimidate me! You shed the blood of my brother on the banks of the Mississippi twenty years ago, and what then? I am here today, thank God, to vindicate the principles baptized in his blood." (Brodie, 1959, pp. 136–137)

4:30 A.M., April 12, 1861 – General Pierre Gustave Toutant Beauregard gives the order to fire upon Fort Sumter. The Civil War begins.

While events conspired to make the conflict inevitable, attitudes in the South hardened around the election of Abraham Lincoln and the incessant demagoguery of the North. The tactics of the North were viewed as offensive and inane. Charles Jones, a rebel soldier, wrote to his parents in April 1861:

> It is today officially announced that our mails are cut off and that there will be henceforth no further communication . . . with the Confederate States . . . Can you imagine a more suicidal, outrageous, and exasperating policy than that inaugurated by the fanatical administration in Washington? The Black Republicans may rave among the cold hills of their native states, and grow mad with entertainment of infidelity, heresies, and false conceptions of a "higher law"; but Heaven forbid that they ever attempt to set foot upon this land of sunshine, of high-souled honor, and of liberty. It puzzles the imagination to conceive the stupidity, the fanaticism, and the unmitigated rascality which impel them to the course which they are now pursuing. (Myers, 1972, p. 665)

When the end to the carnage finally came, there remained two separate realities and perspectives:

T. Morris Chester, a black correspondent with the *Philadelphia Press*, was in Richmond on April 4, 1865:

> The great event after the capture of the city was the arrival of President Lincoln in it . . . The is no describing the scene along the route. The colored population was wild with enthusiasm. Old men thanked God in a very boisterous manner, and old women shouted upon the pavement as high as they had ever done at a religious revival . . . One enthusiastic old Negro woman exclaimed: "I know that I am free, for I have seen Father Abraham and felt him." When the President returned to the flag-ship of Admiral Porter, in the evening, he was taken from the wharf in a cutter. Just as he pushed off, amid the cheering of the crowd, another good old colored female shouted out, "Don't drown Massa Abe, for God's sake!"

But a self-proclaimed "secesh lady" of the South was terrified and appalled. Catherine Ann Devereux Edmonston wrote in her diary:

> April 16, 1865 – How can I write it? How find words to tell what has befallen us? GEN. LEE HAS SURRENDERED! Surrendered the remnant of his noble Army to an overwhelming horde of mercenary Yankee knaves & foreigners . . . Again and again that noble old man with his band of heroes paused & delivered battle, each time with fearful loss to their prisoners, but at length utterly exhausted by fatigue, privation, & incessant fighting, fighting for the last three days continuous near Appomattox Court House he found his rear molested by Thomas with the Army of Tennessee. Utterly unable to cope with this new enemy, his troops already thinned by exhaustion, wounds, death, &, sad to say, desertion, he took the only course left to him and SURRENDERED! . . . We stand appalled at our disaster! What have we done to be thus visited? That LEE, Lee upon whom hung the hopes of the whole country, should be a prisoner seems too dreadful to be realized!
>
> . . . I am utterly paperless. Every letter I possessed, letters which I cherished as my heart's blood . . . all, all destroyed . . .
>
> . . . As the packet consumed [in fire] scarce could I refrain from snatching it from the flames & at least keeping ONE, one of those precious sheets which seemed to me transcripts of our young hearts & young love; but the thought of seeing them in Yankee hands, of hearing them read in vile Yankee drawl amidst peals of vulgar Yankee laughter restrained me . . . (Crabtree, 1979, pp. 694–696)

Foner's assessment:

> . . . Resentment of southern political power, devotion to the Union, anti-slavery based upon the free labor argument, moral revulsion to the peculiar institution [of slavery], racial prejudice, a commitment to the northern social order and its development and expansion—all these elements were intertwined in the Republican world-view. What

they added up to was the conviction that North and South represented two social systems whose values, interests, and future prospects were in sharp, perhaps mortal, conflict with one another. (Foner, 1990, p. 310)

That it was inevitable does not relieve the burden of the other question: was it worth the cost?

Even the most noted historians will not commit themselves on this issue. Stampp writes:

> Precisely when slavery's peaceful end would have come no revisionist could say, but most of them guessed it could have lasted no longer than another generation, or no later than the end of the nineteenth century . . . [but] it would have meant that the four million slaves of 1860, as well as their descendants, would have remained in bondage . . . How to balance the lives of half a million soldiers against the prolonged bondage of four million slaves is a question with profound moral implications. (Stampp, 1980, pp. 221–222)

If you accept the premise that the war was inevitable and, horribly, necessary, then those who fomented the conflict were the most right.

That, of course, is the exact point Lincoln tried to make in the Gettysburg address. His audience wasn't the quaint townspeople of a sleepy Pennsylvania village. He was aiming at the next day's New York Times, at historians, at posterity. In a classic example of spin-meistering, the address was carefully crafted to claim the moral ground that justified the mayhem. It was a brilliant stroke of immediate revisionism.

Whatever the political machinations, whatever the mundane realities that shaped the events leading to the war, generations to come were going to know that the war was really about "government of the people, by the people, and for the people."

This is what salves the Union conscience.

Had Pickett's charge succeeded, President Davis would have come to Gettysburg afterward and, with equal solemnity, declared the inalienable rights of an entire culture to determine its social and economic structure for itself. He would have said that even the (admittedly) evil-sounding institution of servitude was subject to the larger morality of the Southern way of life.

What's more, Jefferson Davis' Gettysburg Address would have been equally high minded in tone, thereby justifying the means of the conflict toward the ends. He would have graciously accepted the Union partisans into the new federal government on Southern terms.

Looking one or two generations ahead, this would have meant vestiges of slavery or at least stubborn racism for years. The genteel aspects of the plantation masking inequality and a cancer that continued to grow sub rosa would be a metaphor for the entire government structure. Henry Ward Beecher, in his eulogy for John Brown, noted: "All other causes of friction, put together, derived from the weakness or the wickedness of men, are not half so mischievous to our land as is this gigantic evil." (Warch, 1973, p. 263)

Slavery was the infection that kept the South from true health. A reversal of fortune in the Civil War would have spread aspects of that disease throughout the economic system of the young nation. It can be argued that the sickness would have struck down the industrial revolution in its prime, and the explosion of progress in the 20th century might have been stillborn in the aftermath of southern ascendancy.

From this perspective, the true stalwarts on both sides were the radicals. They forced the issue. They pushed the nation to the choice. The option of compromise, while practiced by many well-intentioned leaders, would have confused the issue. So it was the activists who, whatever, their motivation, deserve recognition for executing a Civil War than ended slavery and put the nation on a track toward industrialization.

It was Thaddeus Stevens, the Scourge of the South, the Old Commoner, the irascible, imponderable force who stood most defiantly erect in the winds of war.

Back to the fateful year of 1850, Toombs first advocated disunion and was the first to utter the dreaded concept of disunion on the floor of the House: "I do not hesitate to avow, before the House and the country and in the presence of the living God, that if you seek to drive us from California and New Mexico and to abolish slavery in the District of Columbia, I am for disunion. Give me securities that the power you seek will not be used to the injury of my constituents, then you can have my cooperation. Refuse, and as far as I am concerned, let discord reign forever." (Singmaster, 1947, p. 294)

It was Stevens who rose to an inspired response and an assault on slavery. His reputation for fiery oration had preceded him and colleagues were surprised to hear him open with a restrained economic rationale:

> Does slavery contribute to any of these? In the low light of political economy, the answer is no. Slave countries never have many industrious freemen. When the lash is the only stimulant, man revolts from labor. The soil occupied by slavery is much less productive than a similar soil occupied by freemen. Take Virginia—

This was a stunning broadside on the Commonwealth of Presidents, home of the Democrats, land of the gentry, and Jefferson and Washington themselves. Stevens had the undivided attention of the body and went on:

> She has capabilities equal, if not superior to any State of the Union. When the Constitution was adopted, she was the most powerful State. What is she now? Her population is doubled by that of New York. Her land, cultivated by unwilling hands, is not productive. There is scarcely a town within her borders, her ancient villages wear the appearance of mournful decay; her minerals and timber are unwrought, her ports without commerce . . . Virginia, by her own confession, has become a breeder of slaves . . . {they} are compelled to turn to slaveholders for a livelihood . . . (Singmaster, 1947, p. 296)

Then the flourish and the lunge:

> In this (Virginia) Government, the free white citizens are rulers and all other subjects. The subject has no rights, social, political, or

personal. He has no voice in the law; he can hold no property. His very wife and children are not his. His labor is another's. He is not a serf, with half the rights of man, like the subjects of despotic Russia; but a naked slave, stripped of every right God and Nature gave him. The rulers of every despotism are free—Nicholas of Russia, the Grand Sultan of Turkey, the butcher of Austria. Augustus, Antony, and Lepidus were free while they drenched Rome in blood. You and I, and the sixteen million are free, while we rivet manacles on four million of our fellowmen . . .

The reaction from the House was awe and snarls. It was the first of many shots that Stevens would fire across the partisan bow. (Singmaster, 1947, pp. 297–299)

Frederick W. Seward in Reminiscences writes about members hiding from a vote on the Fugitive Slave Bill:

I happened to be in the Congressional Library that morning, when I saw many Northern members coming in, one by one, and aimlessly strolling about. Inquiring of one what was going on in the House, I was told that the Fugitive Slave Law was about to be voted on. Those were the "dodgers" who did not want to vote for it, nor dare to vote against it. I hurried to the House gallery, in time to find Thaddeus Stevens on his feet, and sarcastically moving that the Speaker "send one of his pages to inform the members that they can return with safety, as the slavery question had been disposed of. (Korngold, 1955, p. 91)

In an angry response to a rosy picture painted by Jefferson Davis about slaves and their plantation lives, Stevens declaimed:

Gentlemen on this floor and in the Senate have repeatedly, during this discussion, asserted that slavery was amoral, political, and personal blessing, that the slave was free from care, contented, happy, fat, and sleek . . . Well, if this be so, let us give all a chance to enjoy this blessing. Let the slaves, who choose, go free; and the free, who choose, become slaves . . . Homer informs us that the moment a man becomes a slave, he loses half the man; a few short years of apprenticeship will expunge all the rest except the faint glimmerings of an immortal soul. Take your stand, therefore, courageously in the swamp, spade, and mattock in hand, and uncovered, and half-naked, toil beneath the broiling sun. Go home to your hut at night, and sleep on the bare ground, and go forth in the morning unwashed to give you a color that will pass muster in the most fastidious and pious slave market in all Christendom . . . Deprived of all education, cut off from all ambitions and aspirations, your mind would soon lose all foolish and perplexing desires for freedom; and the whole man would be sunk into a most happy and contented indifference. (Brodie, 1959, p. 109)

Speaker Howell Cobb, after hearing Stevens remarked: "Our enemy has a general now. The man is rich; therefore, we cannot buy him. He does not want higher office; therefore, we cannot allure him. He is not vicious; therefore, we cannot seduce him. He is in earnest. He means what he says. He is bold. He cannot be flattered or frightened." (Brodie, 1959, p. 100)

———

Just his role in the events leading up to the Civil War was enough to place Thaddeus Stevens in everybody's history books. But his most vaunted and criticized moments were yet to come.

CHAPTER FIFTEEN

December 1861

Nearly 15 years after he first proposed the abolition of slavery in a resolution before the nascent Anti-Mason Party, Thaddeus Stevens took to the floor of the U.S. Congress to lead the charge again.

> Whereas slavery has caused the present rebellion in the United States; and whereas there can be no solid and permanent peace and union in this Republic so long as that institution exists within it; and whereas slaves are now used by the rebels as an essential means of supporting and protracting the war; and whereas by the law of nations it is right to liberate the slaves of an enemy to weaken his power; Therefore,
>
> Be it resolved by the Senate and House of Representatives of the United States of America in Congress assembled, That the President be requested to declare free, and to direct all our generals and officers in command to order freedom to all slaves who shall leave their masters, or who shall aid in quelling this rebellion.
>
> SEC. 2. And be it further resolved, That the United States pledge the faith of the Union to make full and fair compensation to all loyal citizens who are and shall remain active in supporting the Union for all the loss they may sustain by virtue of this act. (Palmer, 1997, p. 229)

For Thaddeus Stevens and most of the leaders in Congress, the Civil War was personal. It was common for them to receive letters from the field of battle where brothers, sons, and nephews fought amid unspeakable horrors.

Alanson Stevens fought with the 77th Regiment of Pennsylvania volunteers and arrived at the Battle of Shiloh just after the carnage had occurred. Both sides lost over 10,000 men, and Alanson shared this with his uncle Thad:

> The battlefield was mostly woods and extends over a space of five miles wide, and the length is unknown. It was a desperately contested Battle as everything shows, when we arrived on the field it was literally covered with dead bodies of men and horses for miles . . . I have enjoyed good health all the time with the exception of a slight attack of dysentery . . .

"Dear Nephew," Stevens wrote back, "I am glad to hear that with all your hard work, you are still in good health. I trust nothing worse may befall you . . . Thaddeus [Jr.—his other nephew} is down near the enemy, and a battle seems likely—Let Me hear from you as often as possible."

Thaddeus, Jr. had a larger appetite for politics and couldn't help but share his uncle's frustration with Lincoln's lukewarm position on enforcing emancipation. He wrote on December 4, 1862:

> Dear Uncle, The President's message [offering a compromise for gradual emancipation instead of the immediate freedom that Stevens had called for in his House Resolution] is looked upon here as of little account . . . He is the message proposes to get rid of it [slavery] in thirty years. At the rate we go on, I shall be rejoiced to see slavery abolished in sixty years and doubt if it will be in six hundred . . . I received Mrs. Smith letter . . . William Burton started for home as soon as he heard of his wife's death. I gave him a letter to Mrs. Smith. I hope to hear from you soon. (Palmer, 1997, pp. 292, 329, 330)

Stevens wrote several more times to both soldiers that summer. Alanson was killed at the Battle of Chickamauga in September 1863. Thaddeus Jr. rose to the rank of Lt. Colonel and survived the war.

CHAPTER SIXTEEN

November 1863

At Gettysburg, Abraham Lincoln took his position on the stage between his Secretary of State, William Seward, and the principal speaker for the day, the distinguished President of Harvard, Edward Everett. A former Secretary of State himself, Everett "was that rare thing, a scholar and Ivy-League diplomat who could hold audiences in thrall. His voice, his diction, and gestures were successfully dramatic, and he always performed his carefully written text, no matter how long, from memory." (Wills, p. 24) The national cemetery dedication was built around Everett's schedule who typically needed over a month to prepare one of his famous declamations.

The bunting was draped around the platform and the flags representing those governors in attendance—Bradford of Maryland, Curtin of Pennsylvania, Morton of Indiana, Seymour of New York, Barber of New Jersey, Todd of Ohio—added to what the New York Times would describe as "a solemn and imposing event."

The president settled his bony frame into the wooden chair. The nausea of a days-old virus was subsiding, but his head ached. This neuralgia had become a chronic condition that he was resigned to bear until the rebellion was finally suppressed.

The morning dispatches were not good. General Burnside was holding his own against superior numbers of rebel forces, but Longstreet had inflicted heavy casualties and bought time needed for fortifications by the South in Knoxville. In what had become a daily litany of carnage, Lincoln learned that General Saunders was wounded and that Captain Sikes, whom he knew personally, was in critical condition. About 450 Union soldiers had died in the last 48 hours and, the president knew, the heavy casualties would occur when the blue and gray engaged tomorrow in the battle for Tennessee.

Fifteen thousand citizens crowded the grounds when the president removed his top hat for the invocation. The townsfolk uncovered in unison, a sea of crepe moving in mournful salute. The parade through the town had lasted well over an hour, and Everett was already clearing his throat for what Lincoln knew would be an oration of at least two hours. Reverend Stockton was into a prayer that was already well beyond the length of Lincoln's planned remarks, and the president began to worry about the brevity of his address.

The sun broke through a dense fog as the preacher continued this late November morning. The events of last July and the other fierce realities of the war had etched permanent lines on the face and heart of the president of the United States of America. Before the hostilities erupted, president-elect Lincoln had observed: "There are already among us those, who, IF THE UNION BE PRESERVED, will live to see it contain two hundred and fifty millions." (Lincoln, p. 207) The burden to posterity weighed more heavily on his shoulders today than it ever had.

Since his inauguration, he bore this war as if it were his own personal leprosy. He fumed for a year over McLellan's hesitations. He recalled the April 1862 Peninsular campaign where federal troops advanced ever so slowly on Richmond and then, inexplicably, withdrew north to Harrison's Landing to protect Washington, D.C. Press on to Richmond," demanded the President but McLellan waited too long for reinforcements and lost the opportunity.

(General Lee himself would later dispute Lincoln's strategy. "We would have swapped queens," said Lee. That is, if McLellan had captured Richmond, Lee would have captured Washington. (Lincoln, p. 388) This would have forced the European powers to recognize the Confederacy and may have prolonged, not shortened the war.)

Still, Lincoln fumed as the casualties mounted, and the dispatches and the new photographic techniques of Matthew Brady and Sam Cooley brought continuous reminders. Lincoln remembered an incident as far back as October 1861 in which McLellan, thinking he was outgunned by artillery trained on troops approaching Centerville, Virginia, stopped the attack. Brady's photography revealed the guns to be logs painted and rigged to look like cannons and, thought Lincoln, now the public knew of McLellan's cowardice. It was during that time that Col. Edward Baker, a former Senator from Oregon was killed on the banks of the Potomac. Lincoln had named his second son after Ed Baker, and he wept when he heard the news.

And then there was the incomprehensible loss of his own precious 11-year-old Willie to "bilious fever" in February 1862. In the rage of battles, Abraham and Mary Todd Lincoln kept a sleepless vigil for ten days, and Lincoln grieved openly when his son died: "My poor boy, he was too good for this earth . . . it is hard, hard to have him die!"

But it was on to Shiloh where 100,000 men fought. One in four was a casualty—3,477 died. One historian wrote later: "More than all of the Americans who died in all of the battles of the Revolution, the War of 1812, and the War of Mexico combined[died] at the battle of Shiloh." (Ward, 1994, p. 111).

Days after the Gettysburg battle, a confederate general released official casualty numbers that numbed the minds of both north and south: total killed – 5,664, total wounded – 27,196, total missing – 10,584. (Gallagher, n.d., p. 100)

It is no wonder that Walt Whitman had observed the strain: "I see the president almost every day . . . I see very plainly Abraham Lincoln's dark brown face with its deep cut lines, the eyes always to me with a deep latent sadness. None of the artists or pictures has caught the deep . . . expression of this man's face."

Abraham Lincoln could not have uttered a lengthy speech if he wanted to. He really could not hallow or consecrate the occasion with words any more than those who had fallen had done with blood. Speechifying seemed suddenly in poor taste or at least best left to the learned Mr. Everett. Still, he hoped that the press and public would not construe his brevity as a lack of interest or as a last-minute extemporaneous token. What he had to say was important. He had journeyed from Washington to make his point, but the impenetrable pain of Gettysburg would preclude pomposity—at least for him.

Besides, thought Lincoln, that preacher, Rev. Stockton, is doing a pretty fair job of capturing the moment:

> . . . How little we can do for them! We come with the humility of
> prayer, with the pathetic eloquence of venerable wisdom, with the
> tender beauty of poetry, with the plaintive harmony of music, with
> the honest tribute of Chief Magistrate, and with all these honorable
> attendances; but our best hope is Thy blessings. O Lord, our God,
> bless us. O, our Father, bless the bereaved, whether absent or present.
> Bless our sick and wounded soldiers and sailors. Bless all our rulers
> and people. Bless our army and navy. Bless the efforts to suppress
> this rebellion, and bless all the associations of this day, and place, and
> scene forever.

———

As he looked out upon the bereaved, the mothers and fathers of Gettysburg, Lincoln felt more like Chief Consoler than Chief Magistrate. His mind drifted to earlier battles. He remembered the shock of Shiloh and Vicksburg and Sharpsburg. ✳

———

At the Battle of Sharpsburg, September last, the result was bloody and particularly frustrating. McLellan sat with 95,000 troops to the rebels' 18,000 across Antietam Creek. Instead of thrusting a coordinated attack, he allowed a series of disjointed lunges that resulted in heavy losses with no result. Lee's army had pulled back and, Lincoln, was convinced, the War could have ended had McLellan pursued. Instead, the

President heard still more stories of legendary resolve of southern officers and the war dragged on.

Lincoln thought about Stonewall Jackson, Lee's right-hand man who fell at Chancellorsville. His wife, Anna, broke the news to him that his wounds were fatal. "Doctor," Jackson said, "Anna informs me that you have told her that I am to die today. Is this so?" The doctor nodded. "Very good, very good," said Jackson, "It is alright. My wish is fulfilled; I have always desired to die on Sunday." Whether delirious or inspired, Stonewall Jackson bolted upright at about 3:00 P.M. to exclaim: "Order A.P. Hill to prepare for action! Pass the infantry to the front . . . Let us cross the river and rest under the shade of the trees."

———

For some reason, the President thought that the decisive action here at Gettysburg also happened at about that same time in the afternoon. On July 2, just four months ago, General Meade and General Lee and 150,000 troops exchanged fire all morning. One young General showed either uncommon bravery or recklessness with repeated headlong charges into confederate positions. Custer, Lincoln thought, that was his name. ✻

———

There had been a lull, a morbid calm, like on Golgotha, where Christ himself waited for the end. Meade and his commanders had rested and eaten. Suddenly the skies opened and, not 1,000 feet from where the President now sat, one of the attendants serving butter was cut in two by a shell. General Hancock was already on his horse riding up and down the prophetically named Cemetery Ridge, unflinching, drumming up the courage of his men. "God bless him," thought Lincoln. His retort to attendants who sought to rein him in was: "There are times when a core commander's life does not count!"

After relentless shelling, then quiet from the Union guns, Lee and General Longstreet conferred. Were the Union troops in disarray? Was the silence of the guns real or entrapment? Were the fortifications on

Cemetery Hill and Ridge sufficiently damaged so that their forces could break through?

At the hour when Christ and Stonewall Jackson met death, a frenzied, furious, sea of gray exploded from the trees and flowed uphill. Major George E. Pickett led the charge that could have destroyed the union. One rebel lieutenant cried out: "Home, boys, home! Remember, home is beyond those hills!" Row after row moved forward, now in the open and facing the timeless cruelty of fate and war. Lincoln took no comfort in the fact that Northern discipline and field actions were, for once, outstanding. He knew that Meade had taken the heart out of the rebels' northern surge. He knew that this first assault on the free soil of the north would likely be the last. He knew that the strategic locations of Harrisburg and Philadelphia, the anthracite coal regions of Central Pennsylvania, and the populations in New York and Massachusetts were largely secured. But he knew the cost: almost 50,000 dead, wounded or missing. He knew that hospital tents and mass graves marked Gettysburg for months after the battle and for all times as a monument to strife and ultimate sacrifice. (Ward, 1994, pp. 228–232)

One writer captured the horror from the perspective of a Southern general's aide:

> It is the third of July 1863. Lee's line of battle, stretching along the crest of Seminary Ridge, awaits the signal . . . The infantry are laughing, jesting, cooking their rations, and smoking their pipes. The ragged cannoneers, with flashing eyes, smiling lips, and faces blackened with powder, are standing in groups, or lying down around the pieces of artillery. Near the center of the line, a gray-headed officer, in plain uniform, and entirely unattended, has dismounted and is reconnoitering the Federal position through a pair of field-glasses.
>
> It is Lee, and he is looking toward Cemetery Heights, the Mount St. Jean of the new Waterloo—on whose slopes the immense conflict is going to be decided . . .
>
> The grand assault is about to begin.

That assault is going to be one of the most desperate in all history . . . At Round Top, blood flowed—here the earth is going to be soaked with it . . .

Those two tigers, the army of Northern Virginia and the army of the Potomac, are crouching, and about to spring . . .

Then is a spectacle which will long be remembered with a throb of the heart by many. The thinned ranks of the Virginians are advancing, unmoved, into the very jaws of death. They go forward—and are annihilated. At every step, death meets them. The furious fire of the enemy, on both flanks and in their front, hurls them back, mangled and dying. The brave Garnett is killed while leading on his men. Kemper is lying on the earth, maimed for life. Armistead is mortally wounded at the moment when he leaps upon the breastwork: he waves his hat on the point of his sword, and staggers, and falls. Of fifteen field officers, fourteen have fallen. Three-fourths of the men are dead, wounded, or prisoners. The Federal infantry has closed in on the flanks and rear of the Virginians, the little band is enveloped, and cut off from succor, they turn and face the enemy, bayonet to bayonet, and die.

When the smoke drifts away, all is seen to be over. It is a panting, staggering, bleeding remnant only of the brave division that is coming back so slowly yonder. They are swept from the fatal hill—pursued by yells, cheers, cannon-shot, musket-balls, and canister. As they doggedly retire before the howling hurricane, the wounded are seen to stagger and fall. Over the dead and dying sweeps the canister. Amid volleys of musketry and the roar of cannon, all but a handful of Pickett's Virginians pass into eternity.

It would be more than a year before Lee and Grant would meet at Appomattox. There would be torment and carnage even after the President's benediction today. It would seem like an eternity before Lincoln could hear the collective sigh of relief in the Laus Deo prayer of Whittier:

It is done!
Clang of bell and roar of gun
Send the tidings up and down.

How the belfries rock and reel!
How the great guns, peal on peal,
Fling the joy from town to town!

Ring and swing,
Bells of joy! On morning's wing
Sound the song of praise abroad!

With a sound of broken chains
Tell the nations that He reigns,
Who alone is Lord and God!

(Laus Deo, *American Tradition in Literature*)

———

Abraham Lincoln rose and reached for his whiskered chin.
He was stooped at the shoulders and suddenly calm. In this
place, at this time, it was he who must salvage some meaning from
the holocaust. This town, this battlefield, this sepulcher must be
redeemed. This loftiness of thought and his silent paean to the dead
and devastated absorbed him for a few seconds.

Before murmurs of the crowd could invade the moment, he
straightened his shoulders and swallowed once to speak.

"Four score and seven years ago . . ." just then, without warning
and with complete intrusion into the tone and purpose of the day,
a thought came whistling like a bullet into the President's mind:
"Where the hell is Thaddeus Stevens?

———

Abraham Lincoln shook his wet hands over the porcelain wash-
basin and emerged from the train car lavatory, toweling the water
off his face. The cold splash helped remove the grime of his long day,
and the President allowed himself the luxury of lingering a moment
in the softness of the towel.

"A note, you say?"

Mr. Hay and Mr. Nicolay had waited until after the address to inform the President about Stevens' letter. "Let's have a look at it," said the President.

"Mr. President: I regret that personal convictions prevent my joining you in Gettysburg. Pennsylvania has suffered too much to allow you to continue to suffer fools. Your patient servant, T. Stevens." ✳

———

For Thaddeus Stevens, impertinence to Presidents was part of his nature. He had hounded his constituent, hapless James Buchanan when the 15th President sought accommodation rather than confrontation with the South. He had no use for timidity in the face of the moral outrage he saw in slavery. Had Buchanan listened to Stevens, in the Old Commoner's mind, Ft. Sumter would have been reinforced immediately and mightily, and an impenetrable line with the South would have been drawn. He had said, "encircle the slave states of this Union with free States as a cordon of fire, [so] that slavery, like a scorpion, would sting itself to death." (Brodie, 1959, p. 106)

And Lincoln. Honest Abe. The rail-splitter. In a sense, according to Stevens, Lincoln was worse. Lincoln, at heart, truly opposed slavery and saw it for the indignity and outrage that it was. But he was still not willing to commit himself passionately to the cause. The Proclamation was, according to Stevens, over a year too late, and he knew that it came primarily as an economic and strategic weapon against the South. This champion of the oppressed, this frontiersman who bested the Little Giant himself in the Douglas debates, acted cravenly to use slavery to galvanize the new Republican party around his candidacy and then surrounded himself with advisers who would coddle the miscreants below the Mason-Dixon line. How could we hope to execute a War, how could we eradicate the evil if the President's own Postmaster General continues to give aid and comfort to the enemy?

The three men in the train car knew how pivotal Stevens was to the Northern cause and to rally the Congress for what still lay ahead—not to mention the critical electoral importance of the state of Pennsylvania. That was, at least in part, a reason they were at Gettysburg this day. They also knew, however, the venomous sting of Stevens. Was it not just weeks ago the Old Commoner had made his pronouncement on the President's electability when he was asked about President Lincoln's forthcoming visit to Gettysburg? "It is appropriate for the President to come," said Stevens, "Let the dead bury the dead."

———

In that context, Nicolay offered: "The note is quite respectful for Stevens."

"Not so, Mr. Nicolay," said the President as the setting sun bathed the Pennsylvania landscape in orange and tinged the note in his hand. "In music, the rests are as important as the notes. I'm afraid the Old Commoner shows an uncommon knack for diabolical pause. He wants Blair's head. ✻

———

It was unfortunate that Montgomery Blair, the Postmaster-General, had chosen to speak out on the need for conciliation. It made matters worse that his remarks came just as the Emancipation Proclamation was being prepared. Blair, in Steven's mind, had done a treasonous disservice to the Union by still asserting that slavery was a mere secondary consideration. His message to the South was clear: we will not enforce emancipation on its effective date of January 1, 1863, this is just a morale builder for the sagging fortunes of the Union troops. Not that Blair's position was unusual, indeed, the prevailing mood in the war-weary country was to find a political solution to avoid further fratricide. As radical an editor as Horace Greeley only recently had written that some accommodation must be made to end the bloodshed. Others agreed. But Lincoln and Stevens agreed on at least one thing, the die had been cast, and no compromise would be possible.

It was Blair who drew the lightning from Stevens and his band of radicals in the Congress. And it was Lincoln alone who could remedy the situation and, in the process, strike yet another deal required for the assurance of the Keystone State's vote in the coming election.

"Ah, Pennsylvania," Lincoln thought. Simon Cameron, his own Secretary of War, would not come to Gettysburg either. He was at odds with Pennsylvania Governor Andy Curtin and would not appear on the dais. More accurately, the Secretary insisted upon and was refused a place nearer the President than the Governor for the visual benefit of the voters. Stevens was not as petty but just as demanding. And the problem with all three of them was that he needed their collective strength to carry the populous state. ✹

Stevens would continue to be a firebrand, but Lincoln knew that it was possible to direct that passion productively. In fact, he recalled his first correspondence with Stevens twenty-three years earlier in which he accurately identified him as the most insightful of all the Pennsylvania rascals.

Since that time, Pennsylvania had been a joy and a curse. As he structured his Cabinet in December of 1860, carefully balancing the volatile perspectives of a nation on the brink of war with political favors promised, Lincoln had written to a confidant shortly before his first inauguration that Pennsylvania politicians had given him "more trouble than the balance of the Union, not excepting secession." (Klein, 1980, p. 179)

It was during that time that Stevens most endeared himself to the President-elect with the type of sly candor that Lincoln most appreciated. Lincoln had chosen to accommodate Pennsylvania and to relieve his friend Governor-elect Andrew Curtin of the daily political warfare within his party by moving Simon Cameron from Harrisburg to Washington, to serve as Secretary of War.

The President-elect had received an unflattering report from Congressman Thaddeus Stevens in a private conversation at the White House.

"Why, Mr. Stevens," said Lincoln, you don't think the Secretary would steal, do you?"

"Well, Mr. President," Stevens replied, "I don't think he would steal a red-hot stove."

Cameron heard of this, demanded an apology, and when both men faced the President, Stevens said: "Mr. President, I told you the other day that Mr. Cameron would not steal a red-hot stove. I now take that back." (Korngold, 1955, p. 112)

A trace of a smile worked the corners of Lincoln's mouth. Stevens was right about Cameron. He was right about Blair as well. Montgomery Blair was a Kentucky native who distinguished himself as the Mayor of St. Louis and as a judge before moving to Maryland to practice law. He came to Lincoln's attention when, in 1856, he defended Dred Scott in the U.S. Supreme Court. Blair was a sensible man with an even disposition. Too level-headed perhaps for the realities of war. His signal to the south was more than inappropriate; it was contrary to administration policy and the war effort. Lincoln liked Montgomery Blair, but he knew his lingering hopes for some appeasement had become an embarrassment, and perhaps, just perhaps, Thaddeus Stevens and his cabal would be willing to talk John C. Fremont out of his presidential aspirations for 1864 if Blair was the sacrifice.

––––––––

"Well," said Hay, "Mr. Stevens demands Mr. Blair's head. What do you intend to do?"

"I shall give it to him." said the Emancipator. *

––––––––

William Dennison replaced Montgomery Blair as Postmaster General in 1864.

Because of this political "accommodation," Stevens threw himself into the reelection campaign of Abraham Lincoln and gave one of his most spirited campaign speeches at Philadelphia on October 4, 1864:

Shall we agree for the sake of a disgraceful and precarious peace to enslave four million human beings? Shall we aid to rivet the chains on a whole race of God's children that we may purchase the boon of a temporary peace from triumphant traitors? If we are men, we will resist it to the death . . . Well may every honest man, well may every man who loves God and loves liberty, exclaim, "Thank God for Abraham Lincoln!" Wiser and firmer than his official or officious admirers, he has saved the nation from disgrace; he has rescued liberty from destruction. (Korngold, 1955, p. 229)

CHAPTER SEVENTEEN

November 1864

Stevens stood strongly in the face of a growing tide of Northern leaders who were tiring of the war. He was not shy about being heard whether it was on the House floor, in speeches to his constituents, or contacts with the President.

In November 1864, Benjamin Butler offered his wavering voice to a crowd in New York, stating that "Now is a good time for us once again to hold to the deluded men of the South the olive branch of peace and say to them "Come back, come back now. This is the last time of asking."

Stevens was having none of it and dashed off a note to the President:

Lancaster, November 20, 1864
His Excellency A. Lincoln
Sir
This twaddle about new peace propositions, promulgated by Butler
and others is unwise, and nearly as injurious as when made three
or four months ago, which nearly ruined us—All such feeble stuff
enervates the public—I am happy in believing that you will give no
countenance to such superficial suggestions.

Two weeks later, Stevens smiled when he heard in the President's annual address to Congress: "No attempt at negotiation with the insurgent leader could result in any good. He would accept nothing short of severance of the Union—precisely what we will not and cannot give." (Palmer, 1997, pp. 505, 506)

The matter of proffering some peace proposal lingered as an option as the war shifted in the North's favor. As late as January 5, 1865, Stevens found himself staving off Republicans from New York and other northern states. He was on the verge of shepherding through the 13th amendment and had no time for further distractions from those who would allow any form of slavery at this late hour. Stevens believed that the blood spilled in the war earned freedom for all, and he was in complete agreement with Lincoln on that subject. He said so on the House floor:

> I give the President all honor for his course on this question. Never had a man to decide so important a question under such difficulties. He was obliged to decide it for himself, not only unaided but in the midst of the most distracting counsels. I am disclosing no secret when I state his Cabinet has never been a unit. He could receive no aid from them . . . From the moment the great victory was known, while salvos of cannon were proclaiming to the world the virtue and firmness of the people, the controlling journals of the party . . . joined in urging the President to pursue [détente with the south] . . . We are about to ascertain the national will by another vote to amend the Constitution. If gentlemen opposite will yield to the voice of God and humanity and vote for it, I verily believe the sword of the destroying angel will be stayed and this people will be reunited. (Palmer, 1997, pp. 513, 515)

PART FOUR

Reconstruction

CHAPTER EIGHTEEN

January 1865

Ah, love, let us be true
To one another! for the world, which seems
To lie before us like a land of dreams,
So various, so beautiful, so new,
Hath really neither joy, nor love, nor light,
Nor certitude, nor peace, nor help for pain;
As we are here as on a darkling plain
Swept with confused alarms of struggle and flight,
Where ignorant armies clash by night.
(Abrams, *Norton Anthology*; Arnold, "Dover Beach," p. 1040)

Stevens watched as Congress approved the 13th Amendment on January 31, 1865. The South was in retreat, and northern leaders felt, at last, that they could align themselves with the gentleman from Pennsylvania who never wavered in his insistence that all men are created equal.

There had been a reconciliation between the President and Thaddeus Stevens of late. Perhaps because both suffered personal losses in the war; perhaps because both were wary of holding fast to their convictions; perhaps the life-long passions that burned in both were aging them rapidly.

Lincoln rose to give his Second Inaugural Address and chose to lay down the animus of war. He sought to put the union back together:

"With malice toward none; with charity for all; with firmness in the right, as God gives us to see the right, let us strive on to finish the work we are in; to bind up the nation's wounds; to care for him who shall have borne the battle, and for his widow, and his orphan—to do all which may achieve and cherish a just, and a lasting peace, among ourselves, and with all nations."

Stevens, who had defended the President on the floor of the House just weeks before, was not having it. His work to free the slaves had only passed the Congress. It still required ratification in the states, and Stevens did not see how molly-coddling the plantation owners in the south would help.

He set himself as an example of standing firm in the face of threats and distractions in an unusually personal comment on the House floor:

> . . . When, fifteen years ago, I was honored with a seat in this body,
> it was dangerous to talk about this in situation . . . I did not hesitate
> in the midst of bowie knives, and revolvers and howling demons
> upon the other side of the House, to stand here and denounce this
> infamous institution . . . I claimed the right then, as I claim it now, to
> denounce it everywhere. (Brodie, 1959, p. 204)

He was suffering from the loss of his nephew Alanson and dozens of other war victims. He was still chafing about Jubal's attack on his personal property and believed in restitution—if not for himself for the Union.

Stevens turned to the ever-patient Lydia Smith and exploded.

"Are we to welcome these miscreants back into our house without penalty? What about *our* widows and orphans; what about the national treasure squandered in a treasonous war by these traitors and racists?"

Lydia knew that Thaddeus was capable of great compassion, but what was rising in him at this moment was pure anger. It was clear that the twilight of his career would be no different than the see-saw of passion that marked his entire life. ✻

CHAPTER NINETEEN

April 1865

Abraham Lincoln was shot on Good Friday, and died the next day, April 15, 1865.

The unworldly darkness of the moment was captured by Secretary of the Navy, Gideon Welles who was at the President's deathbed:

> "The giant sufferer lay extended diagonally across the bed, which was not long enough for him . . . his slow, full respiration lifted the clothes with each breath that he took. His features were calm and striking . . . About once an hour, Mrs. Lincoln would repair to the bedside of her dying husband with lamentation and tears until overcome by emotion." At 7:22 AM, it was Secretary of War, Edwin Stanton, who pronounced: "Now he belongs to the ages." (Morrison, 1972, pp. 496, 497)

Lincoln lived just long enough to savor Lee's surrender at Appomattox but not nearly long enough to guide his vision of reunification through the Congress.

Stevens wasted no time in stepping into the void. It began with a short letter to the 17th President of the United States:

St. Lawrence Hotel
Philadelphia, Pennsylvania
July 6, 1865
His Excellency Andrew Johnson
I am sure you will pardon me for speaking to you with a candor to
which men in high places are seldom accustomed. Among all the
leading Union men of the North with whom I have had intercourse,
I do not find one who approved of your policy. They believe that
"Restoration" as announced by you will destroy our party (which is
of but little consequence) and will greatly injure the country. Can
you not hold your hand and wait the action of Congress and in the
meantime govern them by military rulers? Profuse pardoning will also
greatly embarrass Congress if they should wish to make the enemy
pay the expenses of the war or a part of it.
With great respect, your obt svt
Thaddeus Stevens

On September 7, 1865, in an address in Lancaster, Pennsylvania,
Stevens set the stage for the confrontation that was to begin with an out-
line of his vision for reconstruction. Far from welcoming the Southern
states back into the family, he urged that they be treated like conquered
territories and that reparations and other considerations had to be met
before they could rejoin the union. It was a far cry from "malice toward
none." (See the full Reconstruction Address in the Appendix).

By the end of the year, the Country had ratified the 13th amendment. Elimination of the cancer of slavery would have been a career
achievement for most leaders. Stevens was not satisfied. His plan was for
a stern, Congress-driven solution for reconstruction, and he managed to
get himself appointed the Chair of both the Appropriations Committee
and the newly formed Joint Committee on Reconstruction. Nobody in
Washington, except for the President, doubted who had taken charge.

CHAPTER TWENTY

February 1866

Ambition should be made of sterner stuff.
 —William Shakespeare, *Julius Caesar*, Act III, Scene II

In the winter of discontent that was 1866, the President reasserted himself with vetoes of bills relating to the funding the "Freedmen's Bureau" and Civil Rights bill, but he would soon find himself accepting four separate Reconstruction Acts that the Congress placed before him.

Andrew Johnson was the object of suspicion and outright derision by many in Congress. This derived from the fact that he was from the "secesh" state of Kentucky and his unsteady entrance on the national scene.

Lincoln had deliberately chosen a "neutral" party for his Vice President but was unaware of Johnson's demons. This was despite a blunt warning from Stevens: "Mr. President, Andrew Johnson is a rank demagogue, and I suspect at heart a damned scoundrel." (Brodie, 1959, p. 217)

Johnson was drunk on the day he was sworn in as Vice President, and he was subsequently regarded lightly by the Congress, if at all.

The Senate Historical Office pulls no punches about the event:

Vice President-elect Andrew Johnson arrived in Washington ill from typhoid fever. The night before his March 4, 1865, inauguration, he fortified himself with whiskey at a party hosted by his old friend,

Secretary of the Senate John W. Forney. The next morning, hungover and confronting cold, wet, and windy weather, Johnson proceeded to the Capitol office of Vice President Hannibal Hamlin, where he complained of feeling weak and asked for a tumbler of whiskey. Drinking it straight, he quickly consumed two more. Then, growing red in the face, Johnson entered the overcrowded and overheated Senate Chamber. After Hamlin delivered a brief and stately valedictory, Johnson rose unsteadily to harangue the distinguished crowd about his humble origins and his triumph over the rebel aristocracy. In the shocked and silent audience, President Abraham Lincoln showed an expression of "unutterable sorrow," while Senator Charles Sumner covered his face with his hands. Former Vice President Hamlin tugged vainly at Johnson's coattails, trying to cut short his remarks. After Johnson finally quieted, took the oath of office, and kissed the Bible, he tried to swear in the new senators, but became so confused that he had to turn the job over to a Senate clerk.
(https://www.senate.gov/artandhistory/history/common/generic
  /Senate_Historical_Office.htm)

Still, Johnson saw it as his mission to restore the Southern states to the Union. If anything, he was intent on a faster reconciliation than even Lincoln had envisioned. The new President's first executive orders had already caused resentment in the north and confusion in the south. Stevens, now invoking Lincoln as a guide used the martyred President's own words to argue against hasty readmission for any of the rebel states:

> By general law, life AND limb must be protected; yet often a limb
> must be amputated to save a life, but a life is never wisely given to
> save a limb. (Korngold, 1955, p. xi)

Thaddeus Stevens set out to systematize the post-war reconciliation. It was the Stevens resolution that established a joint committee of the Congress "to inquire into the condition of the States which formed the so-called Confederate States of America, and report whether they or any of them are entitled to be represented in either House of Congress. (Woodley, 1937, p. 313)

Stevens, of course, installed the most capable leader he knew as the head of the new Committee on Restoration—himself.

Meanwhile, President Andrew Johnson continued to paint a picture of benevolent progress. He declared in August 1866 that the insurrection was at an end and that "peace, order, tranquility, and civil authority now exist in and throughout the whole of the United States." (Morrison, 1972, p. 506)

His war with Congress, however, was just beginning. He found himself receiving increasing venom from the Radical Republicans who were now taking their cues from Stevens.

CHAPTER TWENTY-ONE

March 1867

Thaddeus Stevens met with his Senate counterpart and fellow Radical Republican, Ben Wade of Ohio. The two concocted a strategy that was brilliant and diabolical.

Their view was that Johnson was not complying with the dictates of Congress on Reconstruction and was a threat to their party and the nation. They sought to control appointees, provisional governors, and other appointments to assure that those appointees were aligned with their cause.

"A Tenure of Office Bill?" asked Wade.

"Indeed," said Stevens, "it would require the advice and consent of the Senate for any appointment and any removal from office that this President or any future President makes."

Wade: "But wouldn't that make the executive branch wholly subservient to the Congress? Like the British Prime Minister's Cabinet presently reports to the House of Commons?"

"Indeed," said Stevens.

The Constitutional conspiracy aside, the men had an ulterior motive. Secretary of War Edwin Stanton was considered an ally of the Radicals in Congress and a possible Presidential candidate. The Tenure of Office Bill would almost certainly force the President's hand to remove Stanton to test the matter's constitutionality before the Supreme Court as quickly as possible.

"But what of Stanton?" asked Wade.

"It is of little consequence," said Stevens. "When the President acts on Stanton, we will bring articles of impeachment. Upon conviction, the President Pro-Tempore of the Senate assumes the office. That, my friend, is you."

The plan was set. ✳

――――――

The Tenure of Office Bill passed in March 1867, and President Johnson immediately asked for the resignation of Edwin Stanton. The Secretary of War barricaded himself in his office, and the House of Representatives began the inquiry into the impeachment of the President.

At one point in the impeachment debate, Stevens took to the floor armed with an article that had been published previously in the New York World. He used it like a sword to wound Johnson and anyone who supported him:

> The drunken and beastly Caligula, the most profligate of Roman emperors, raised his horse to the dignity of consul, an office that in former times had been filled by the greatest warriors and statesmen of the Republic, the Scipios and Catos, and by the mighty Julius himself. The consulship was scarcely more disgraced by that scandalous transaction than is our Vice Presidency by the late election of Andrew Johnson. That office has been adorned in better days by the talents and accomplishments of Adams and Jefferson, Clinton and Gerry, Calhoun and Van Buren. And now to see it filled by this insolent, drunken brute, in comparison with whom even Caligula's horse was respectable, for the poor animal did not abuse its own nature! And to think that only one frail life stands between this insolent clownish drunkard and the Presidency!! May God bless and spare Abraham Lincoln and the United States of America. (Woodley, 1937, p. 315)

CHAPTER TWENTY-TWO

February 1868

Impeachment – The House

Stevens was already the Chairman of the all-powerful Joint Committee on Reconstruction and proceeded to set his own pace for a gradual transition to post-war-normalcy. While critics claimed that his real focus was on harassment of the President, Stevens maintained that it was the proper and necessary exercise of legislative authority that kept a reckless President in check.

President Johnson defied the Committee and ignored the Tenure of Office Act playing into the hands of the "dictator of the Congress." On February 22, 1868, Thaddeus Stevens, now weathered by a lifetime of political and personal battles took once more to the floor:

> With bagging clothes that loosely draped his bent frame, he hobbled in the door behind the Speaker's desk to take his seat. The noise in the galleries subsided; talking on the floor ceased, and a silence fell over the chamber . . . Pale and thoroughly spent, but with a penetrating eye that had not lost its luster, Stevens, in low voice said simply, "I am directed by the Committee on Reconstruction to present to the House a report with an accompanying resolution which I ask the Clerk to read "That Andrew Johnson, President of the United States,

be impeached of high crimes and misdemeanors in office. (Woodley, 1937, p. 393)

Thaddeus Stevens . . . the crippled, fanatical personification of the extremes of the Radical republican movement, master of the house of representatives, with a mouth like the thin edge of an ax warned both houses of congress coldly: "Let me see the recreant who would vote to let such a criminal escape. Point me to one who will dare to do it, and I will show you one who will dare the infamy of posterity. (Kennedy, 1964, p. 110)

Even in these last days, in the words that still shot like arrows from his mouth, Stevens struck the nerves of Southern editors like Edward A. Pollard:

There is a hideous significance about this old man, preparing in the last moments of his own life new instruments of torture for the South, and grinning over the work of his bony and unsightly hands, at the very side of his own grave . . . a picture of diabolism at which the heart shudders. (Brodie, 1959, p. 301)

CHAPTER TWENTY-THREE

March–May 1868

Impeachment – The Senate

Stevens summoned the strength to argue for the articles of impeachment in the weeks ahead but was in no condition to rally the votes needed for conviction in the Senate. Instead, he watched the proceedings intermittently and aided in the overt tactics to pressure wavering members of the Senate. Ninety years later, a young Senator John F. Kennedy would write in *Profiles in Courage*:

> . . . As the trial progressed, it became increasingly apparent that the impatient Republicans did not intend to give the President a fair trial on the formal issues upon which the impeachment was drawn, but intended instead to depose him from the White House on any grounds, real or imagined, for refusing to accept their policies. Telling evidence in the President's favor was arbitrarily excluded. Prejudgment on the part of most Senators was brazenly announced. Attempted bribery and other forms of pressure were rampant. (Kennedy, 1964, p. 113)

The body was comprised of fifty-four members, and eighteen of them had already indicated that they would support the embattled Andrew Johnson. This meant that the Republicans needed to hold every one of the remaining thirty-six votes if they were to achieve the necessary two-thirds majority for conviction.

The Republicans were taken aback to hear that Edmund G. Ross of Kansas was wavering. The freshman Senator had won the seat after his predecessor, Jim Lane, took his own life—after taking a pro-Johnson stand. Indeed, Ross had led a rally in Kansas and whipped Lane's constituents into a hateful frenzy that left Lane mentally and physically broken and may have brought on his suicide.

Ross's credentials with the abolitionists and with the hardline Republicans were strong. He had helped secure freedom for fugitive slaves in the 1850s; he joined the chorus of leaders to keep Kansas a "free" state; he even fought with a militia to repel an armed group of pro-slavers who attempted to invade Kansas. With the high-profile attack on the unfortunate Jim Lane, Ross secured the political backing of the Republicans and the Senate seat.

Surely Edmund Ross would join the Radical Republicans in their coup.

To make sure, Ross received a never-ending stream of proffered emoluments and threats. He was followed in his district and Washington. The New York Tribune reported that Ross was "mercilessly dragged this way and that by both sides, hunted like a fox night and day and badgered by his own colleagues." (Kennedy, 1964, p. 116).

One story is that he received an offer of $20,000 to side with the Radical Republicans. He still didn't budge, and the vociferous Ben Butler remarked: "There is a bushel of money! How much does the damned scoundrel want?"

There was one final telegram from home: "Kansas has heard the evidence and demands the conviction of the President." [signed] D.R. Anthony and 1,000 Others

Ross took the time to send this reply:

> To D.R. Anthony and 1,000 Others: I do not recognize your right
> to demand that I vote either for or against conviction. I have taken
> an oath to do impartial justice according to the Constitution and

laws, and trust that I shall have the courage to vote according to the dictates of my judgment and for the highest good of the country. [signed] —E.G. Ross

———

Thaddeus Stevens was intent on making one last effort to cajole the vote from Senator Ross, and he approached him off the floor of the Senate.

"A word, Senator Ross?"

Ross was exhausted and about to make the most important decision of his life. He thought about ignoring Stevens but was aware of the legendary malice that he would face if he did so.

"Yes, Mr. Stevens?"

"Are you with us on conviction?"

Moments before the roll call was to begin, Ross was still uncertain. "I do not know," he replied.

Stevens felt the surge of contempt building in him. This was a final encounter with a colleague who might not bend under the pressure of his inquisition. It was the culmination of a lifetime of passion for causes that brought freedom to slaves, education to the masses, and expansion of the nation to its "manifest destiny." It also brought Stevens to the fore of misadventures that persecuted Free Masons and other enemies, took the entire Pennsylvania government to a dangerous standstill in the Buckshot War, and abetted in the rise and fall of political leaders with a ferocity that was always borne on the edge of love and hate.

This time was different. Ross, Stevens believed, was an honorable man. This thought tempered his rage as Stevens made his case: "You will, of course, sacrifice your career and be burned in the fires of history if you vote for this pathetic President," said the Old Commoner.

"Maybe so," said Ross, "but I suspect that your passion has clouded your reason on this matter. The times and my country demand that I face the fire and act with the icy detachment of justice."

The steel blue in Thaddeus Stevens' eyes had clouded a bit over the years. His intimidating style was muted somewhat by the faltering way he walked or even attempted to stand. Perhaps it was the ebbing of the life force of the "Dictator of the House" that rendered him less effective than when he dealt with foes as far back as Lancaster and Gettysburg. Perhaps it was that Edmund Ross, a much younger man with his passions and ideals, was capable of rising about the threats and rhetoric to think for himself.

The issue, after all, was nothing less than bringing down the President of the United States. Ross knew that the stakes were even higher than that. Unseating Johnson would send a message to the Southern States that was unmistakable: you are conquered territories subject to the whims of a vindictive cadre of inquisitors in the United States Congress. Ross, like many historians afterward, felt that the country was on the edge of a second civil war.

In the short exchange with Ross, Stevens felt an unusual sensation begin to well up inside of him—doubt. He was unaccustomed to this feeling because of his fierce self-reliance over the years. He was convinced that he was right in all his causes and his personal life choices. He braved his enemies with steadfast confidence in his abilities. He was capable of great mischief but also of great love.

In the last encounter with destiny, in this talk with the beleaguered Edmund Ross, he thought of Lincoln, Buchanan, Cameron, and cabinet members, Governors and newspaper editors, and, finally, Dinah and Lydia Smith.

"Our martyred President called upon all of us to be guided by the better angels of our nature," Ross said.

After a pause, Thaddeus Stevens replied: "So he did, so he did." ✻

———

So it was that the roll call in the Senate began with Ross's vote still uncertain.

The Chief Justice, presiding over the trial in the Senate, called for Ross's vote.

> Every eye was upon the freshman Senator from Kansas. The hopes and fears, the hatred and bitterness of past decades were centered upon this one man. (Kennedy, 1964, p. 118)

In his own words, Ross recorded later that: "I almost literally looked down into my own grave. Friendships, position, fortune, everything that makes life desirable to an ambitious man were about to be swept away by the breath of my mouth."

"Not guilty" was his vote.

Ross and every Republican Senator who sided with the President lost their seats and faced brutal personal and political attacks. It was not until twenty years later, just before Ross's death, that the Kansas newspapers reported on the significance and courage of that vote.

"By the firmness and courage of Senator Ross, the country was saved from calamity greater than war . . . He acted for his conscience and with lofty patriotism, regardless of what he knew must be the ruinous consequences to himself."

Stevens died within months of that vote. The modest surroundings of his final resting place were intentional. His own words on the stone leave a Stevensesque statement of egalitarianism that lives on:

> I repose in this quiet and secluded spot, not from any natural preference for solitude, but finding other cemeteries limited by charter rules as to race, I have chosen this that I might illustrate in death the principles which I advocated through a long life, Equality of man before his Creator.

Thaddeus Stevens lingered on his deathbed, surrounded by several Sisters of Mercy at a hospital in Washington DC. Lydia Smith had taken her up her post as chief comforter and assisted in summoning the "better angels of our natures" as he lay dying.

Stevens touched her hand and surrendered his lifetime of pain and joy and a fierce passion to her and those angels.

> By the fine, fine wind that takes its course through the chaos of the
> world
> Like a fine, an exquisite chisel, a wedge blade inserted;
> If only I am keen and hard like the sheer tip of a wedge
> Driven by invisible blows,
> The rock will split, we shall come at the wonder, we shall find the
> Hesperides.
> Oh, for the wonder that bubbles in my soul,
> I would be a good fountain, a good wellhead,
> Would blur no whisper, spoil no expression.
> What is the knocking?
> What is the knocking at the door in the night?
> It is somebody wants to do us harm.
> No, no, it is the three strange angels.
> Admit them, admit them.
> (D. H. Lawrence, *The Faber Book of Modern Verse*)

Epilogue

Ah, but a man's reach should exceed his grasp,
Or what's a heaven for?
                                    —Robert Browning, "Andrea del Sarto"

Speak of me as I am . . . one who loved not wisely but too well.
                                    —Shakespeare, *Othello*, Act V, Scene II

Fawn Brodie, an early biographer of Stevens, has this final word:

> The malice and hatred in Stevens served to enhance the penetrating
> power of his ideas. His ruthlessness and fire won him a far wider
> audience than mild men usually get. Indignation served him instead
> of love, and a sense of injustice was his substitute for hope. (Brodie,
> 1959 pp. 373–374)

A loftier view was expressed by William Robinson, a New York Democrat:

> He seemed like an eagle, perched alone upon a blasted oak in sullen
> and defiant majesty, scorning alike the chatter and the scream of other
> birds around him; his eye sometimes seemingly covered with film as
> of down from the passing wing of death, but in a moment shooting
> into pinions on which he proudly soared to the sun. That proud and
> defiant spirit, often fierce, sometimes unforgiving, and always bold
> and honest, has passed away.

Chronology

4 Apr 1792	T. Stevens born
1794	Talleyrand in N. England (again?)
1809/1810	T. Stevens at Peacham Academy
1812	Cow incident, Burlington
1812	Father Joshua killed in 1812 War
1814	Lydia Hamilton Smith born in Gettysburg
June 14	T. Stevens graduates from Dartmouth
1815	T. Stevens from Vermont to Pennsylvania
1815	Blackballed from York Co. Bar
Aug 16	Passes Bar in Maryland
Sept 16	Law office opened in Gettysburg
June 17	1st Famous murder case (James Hunter insanity defense)
1820	Missouri Compromise
1821	Charity Butler slave case
1822	Dobbins Trial
May 22	T. Stevens elected to Gettysburg Borough Council
1823	First public anti-slavery speech
1824	Reelected G-Burg Council
23 Sep 24	Dinah murder (letters begin)
1826	T. Stevens opens ironworks (half-owner of Maria Works)
25 July 26	T. Stevens first public speech supporting public education
Sep 26	Wm. Morgan murdered (Anti-Masonry launched)
Mar 30	T. Stevens, John Ingram publish the *Star and Banner* (Adams Co. Anti-Masonic Newspaper)
8 June 30	Jacob LeFever, *Gettysburg Compiler* revives Dinah murder
10 Aug 30	LeFever attacks on Dinah again
1831	T. Stevens left bald by typhoid

1831	T. Stevens opens Mifflin forge
1831	T. Stevens meets Wm. H. Seward at Anti-Mason convention. Supports Wm. Wirt over Jackson.
1831	Wm. Lloyd Garrison publishes *The Liberator* in Boston
June 31	T. Stevens strongest anti-mason speech to date
June 31	Compiler attack on Stevens draws lawsuit
Aug 31	Nat Turner incident
30 Aug 31	Stevens wins slander suit ($50 fine, three months in jail)
1832	Keziah suicide incident (found by Mrs. Hamilton Lydia's mother)
1832	Presidential politics: Jackson/Clay/Wirt
1832	Seward joins Clay in Whig Party, Stevens stays with Wirt
1832	Gettysburg College chartered
Nov 33	T. Stevens elected to the legislature
1834	launches Anti-Mason investigation
1834	secures $18,000 appropriation for Gettysburg College
1834	Common Schools law passed
1835	Anti-Mason coalition seizes the majority in Pennsylvania House, Senate, and Governorship
11 Apr 35	Schools repeal vote in House, Stevens speech saves public education
Aug 35	trial on Freemasonry disposed of finally (Stevens awarded $1800)
Nov 35	reelected to legislature
Dec 35	Jackson denounces abolitionists (confirms Democrat/South coalition)
11 Jan 36	Anti-Mason hearings by Stevens
21 Jan 36	Hearings, investigations completed
1836	Blanchard advice to Stevens: turn anti-Mason fervor to anti-slavery
1836	So. editors advertise to kidnap abolitionist leaders, incl. Stevens
1836	Van Buren elected President
1836	Buchanan elected to U.S. Senate
1837	opens Caledonia forge
1837	Pennsylvania Constitutional Convention
1837	Panic and Specie Circular

1837	Close of Maria furnace
Nov 37	reelected to legislature
Nov 37	Porter elected Gov., Ritner (Anti-Mason contests with Stevens et al.)
1838	Whittier's office sacked and burned in Philadelphia
1838	State Banks' charter renewals bring bribery charges. Stevens plan to pay for schools.
1838	brief encounter with Robert Smith's daughter
Jan 38	Buckshot War, Porter remains Gov. (Stevens strategy squashed after 5 Whig Pennsylvania Senators cave in)
Feb 38	storms out after Buckshot War
May 38	returns to House (Hopkins, D-Speaker)
1840	Whigs led by Henry Clay, Harrison wins with T. Stevens' support (Postmaster-General offered to Stevens then retracted)
27 Dec 40	double-crossed by Harrison
Jan 42	renounces politics, law in Lancaster works to pay off business debts
Nov 44	Henry Clay leads "conscience fringe" of Whigs.
Nov 46	Wilmot Proviso
1848	death of Isaac Smith; T. Stevens retains Lydia as housekeeper. Lydia - 35, T.S. - 56
1848	Wm. H. Seward, Salmon P. Chase on national scene
Nov 48	T. Stevens elected to Congress as Whig (represents Lancaster) receives 27 votes for Speaker in factionalized House on his first day
1849	H.D. Thoreau writes Civil Disobedience
1850	Fugitive Slave Law enhanced
1850	Z. Taylor (anti-slavery) dies in office, Millard Fillmore appoints Webster to State
20 Feb 50	T. Stevens speaks out against slavery
7 Mar 50	Webster supports Clay/Douglas compromise opposes abolitionists) in Seventh of March Speech
10 June 50	another anti-slavery speech on the floor
Nov 50	re-elected to Congress
1851	Sumner replaces Webster as Mass. Senator
11 Sept 51	Christiana Slave Riots

1852	Whigs shattered after set-backs, loss of Clay
Nov 52	T. Stevens defeated after defending Christiana participants
1854	Kansas Nebraska bill gives rise to Rep. party
Nov 54	T. Stevens flirtation with American Party (Know-Nothings)
Nov 55	Stevens joins Republicans
22 May 56	Sumner physically beaten on Senate floor
Nov 56	Buchanan defeats John C. Fremont (Fillmore split votes of anti-Democrats)
Nov 57	Dred Scott decision
1858	Harper's Ferry
Apr 58	Brother Joshua dies
Nov 58	Stevens Returns to Congress (Lincoln loses to Douglas in Ill.) Takes Lydia with him at age 67
1859	Keitt/Stevens exchange on floor leads to knives
2 Dec 59	John Brown lynched
1860	skirmishes in Congress
1860	Crittenden (Kentucky) offers final compromise (sons served North and South)
5 Apr 60	Owen Lovejoy speech
Nov 60	Stevens reelected, Lincoln elected President
July 61	Stevens Act frees slaves engaged in War activities
Sept 61	Lincoln, cautious, draws Stevens' fire
Nov 61	Stevens drafts total emancipation proclamation
Dec 61	Stevens proposes emancipation with compensation to owners
Dec 61	Lincoln in message to Congress proposes phase-out of slavery in border states by 1900. Stevens scoffs.
12 Jan 62	Stevens notes 150,000 Negro troops
Mar 62	Lincoln calls for voluntary emancipation in border states. Stevens scoffs.
13 Mar 62	Stevens bill forbidding armed forces to return fugitive slaves.
5 Sept 62	Stevens speech despairing about freeing the slaves
Nov 62	Stevens reelected
1 Jan 63	Emancipation Proclamation
June 63	Caledonia works burnt by rebels en route to Gettysburg
July 63	Battle of Gettysburg
Aug 63	Stevens pushes Lincoln on Montgomery Blair

21 Sept 63	Alanson Stevens (nephew) dies
Nov 63	Gettysburg Address
Mar 64	Stevens and Cameron consulted by Lincoln on Hamlin replacement. Stevens objects to Johnson as VEEP
4 July 64	Wade-Davis passes, pocket-vetoed by Lincoln
Nov 64	Stevens reelected; Lincoln reelected
31 Jan 65	13th amendment passes – 119-56
4 Mar 65	Lincoln/Johnson inaugurated
9 Apr 65	Lee surrenders to Grant at Appomattox
14 Apr 65	American flag raised over Ft. Sumter (exactly four years after Sumter loss)
14 Apr 65	Lincoln shot at Ford's Theater
15 Apr 65	Lincoln dies at 7:22 A.M.
Nov 66	strong Rep. victories, including Stevens
1867	Stevens purchases non-segregated plot
1867	niece Lizzie Stevens dies
1867	40th Congress convenes
1868	correspondence with J. Blanchard – frank discussion of morality
16 May 68	Senate vote on impeachment of Johnson (19-35), Conviction failed by one vote.
11 Aug 68	T. Stevens, with nephew Thaddeus and two nuns of charity, baptized
11 Aug 68	Stevens dies just before midnight

Remarks of H. C. A. Brooks of Peacham on the Commemoration of the 100th Anniversary of the Academy

(On Thaddeus Stevens being coerced into an apology to the Peacham Board of Directors)

"Thaddeus Stevens . . . yielded only because he could do nothing else, but it was probably the last time his imperial will ever bowed to the will of man."

Poor, lame, his only support his hardworking mother, his one overmastering, burning desire was to secure an education.

He completed his fit, but never forgot his chagrin. I used to hear the older men of this town, who knew him well, say that after he reached national renown, although they often invited him, they never could get him back to Peacham to make a speech. Poor Thad! Even when he was undergoing the humiliating of signing that paper in the presence of those hard-hearted, uncompromising Trustees, pledging himself never more to act a part in any tragedy at the Academy, there had already been decreed in the mind and will of Omnipotence one of the most awful tragedies of human history, and in that tragedy, Thaddeus Stevens was destined to act a leading part on a stage of which not America alone, but all the world, were to be spectators. After leaving college, as soon as he could earn his way, he prepared himself for the bar and made the great state of Pennsylvania his home. In the political ground-swells of that State we finally see him in the Legislature.

His poverty, his early struggles, and his hard lot taught him to make his life one constant, never-ceasing battle on behalf of the weak, downtrodden and oppressed of every race and color. His career in the Legislature was at the time when Pennsylvania was in the formative state in regard to her educational system. Stevens at once espoused the cause of the youth and the public school . . .

I have called him headstrong, willful. He cared nothing for the conventionalities of life . . . the Lord had to finish with him what the Trustees had failed wholly to accomplish . . .

1849 found our boy who could never again play in any tragedies, comedies and other theatrical parts by candlelight here in Peacham, in the House of Representatives of the Thirty-First Congress. There were giants in those days in the American Congress. For nearly two decades he was associated with the greatest intellects this country has ever produced . . . There he met Webster, Clay, Calhoun, that great triumvirate. There he counseled with Chase, Hale, Hamlin, Seward, Sumner, Giddings, Garfield and Blaine. There he antagonized such men as Soule, Stephens, Davis, Toombs, and Cobb. He was the peer of them all, and he knew it. The North and the South were about to submit to the arbitrament of war the question of African slavery which human argument could never settle. The tragedy was ready. The stage was ready. There being no Trustees to say him nay, Stevens was ready. The first shot fired in 1861 upon the Stars and Stripes rang up the curtain.

Stevens hated slavery with a hatred that verged on madness . . . Every arrow of ridicule, wit, sarcasm, or invective from his twanging bow was aimed straight at the threat of the black monster . . .

Every morning during those four red-hot years of war and grief and blood, Congress watched to see what the "performance" of the great Commoner was to be. Every evening the daily papers were scanned, here in Peacham, by gray-haired men to see what "performance" of their old schoolmate "Thad" had been the day before in the Congress . . .

What a spectacle for gods and men to see the great Commoner, now an old, gray-headed man, feeble, tottering on the brink of the grave, drag the recreant Andrew Johnson from the highest position on earth to the bar of the American Senate, and there to impeach him of high crimes and misdemeanors. His last part was to see the last three amendments to the Constitution practically assured. Then the curtain fell. The tragedy was ended. His life work done." (Brooks statement from Adams Co. Histo. Society)

Stevens on "Free Schools"

Excerpts from State Rep. Thaddeus Stevens' April 11, 1835, speech in defense of the Free Schools Act of 1834.

> It would seem to be humiliating to be under the necessity, in the 19th century, of entering into a formal argument to prove the utility, to free governments, the absolute necessity of education . . . Such necessity would be degrading to a Christian age and a free republic. If then, education be of admitted importance to the people under all forms of governments, and of unquestioned necessity when they govern themselves, it follows of course that its cultivation and diffusion is a matter of public concern and a duty which every government owes to its people . . .
>
> If an elective republic is to endure for any great length of time, every elector must have sufficient information, not only to accumulate wealth and take care of his pecuniary concerns, but to direct wisely the legislatures, the ambassadors, and the executive of the nation—for some part of all these things, some agency in approving or disapproving of them falls to every freeman. If then, the permanency of our government depends upon such knowledge, it is the duty of government to see that the means of information be diffused to every citizen. This is a sufficient answer to those who

deem education a private and not a public duty—who argue that they are willing to educate their own children, but not their neighbor's children . . .

Pennsylvania has half a million children, who either do or ought to go to school six months in the year. . . . If they do not go when they are able, their parents deserve to be held in disgrace. Where they are unable, if the state does not furnish the means, she is criminally negligent . . .

Many complain of the school tax, not so much on account of its amount, as because it is for the benefit of others and not themselves . . . Why do they not urge the same objection against all other taxes? The industrious, thrifty, rich farmer pays a heavy county tax to support criminal courts, build jails, and pay the sheriffs and jailkeepers, and yet probably he never has had any direct personal use for either . . . He cheerfully pays the tax which is necessary to support and punish convicts but loudly complains of that which goes to prevent his fellow being from becoming a criminal, and to obviate the necessity of those humiliating institutions . . .

I trust that when we come to act on this question, we shall all take the lofty ground—look beyond the narrow space which now circumscribes our vision—beyond the passing, fleeting point of time on which we stand; and so cast our votes that the blessing of education shall be conferred on every son of Pennsylvania, shall be carried home to the poorest child of the poorest inhabitant of your mountains so that even he may be prepared to act well his part in this land of freemen.

Stevens on Reconstruction – To the Citizens of Lancaster, Sept. 6, 1865

FELLOW-CITIZENS: In compliance with your request, I have come to give my views of the present condition of the rebel States—of the proper mode of reorganizing the government, and the future prospects of the republic. During the whole progress of the war, I never for a moment felt doubt or despondency. I knew that the loyal North would conquer the rebel despots who sought to destroy freedom. But since that traitorous confederation has been subdued, and we have entered upon the work of "reconstruction" or "restoration," I cannot deny that my heart has become sad at the gloomy prospects before us.

Four years of bloody and expensive war, waged against the United States by eleven States, under a government called the "Confederate States of America," to which they acknowledged allegiance, have overthrown all governments within those States which could be acknowledged as legitimate by the Union. The armies of the Confederate States having been conquered and subdued, and their territory possessed by the United States, it becomes necessary to establish governments therein which shall be republican in form and principles and form a "more perfect Union" with the parent government. It is desirable that such a course should be pursued as to exclude from those governments every vestige of human bondage, and render the same forever impossible in this nation; and to take care that no principles of self-destruction shall be incorporated therein. In effecting this, it is to be hoped that no provision of the Constitution will be infringed, and no principle of the law of nations disregarded. Especially must we take care that in rebuking this unjust and treasonable war, the authorities of the Union shall indulge in no acts of usurpation which may tend to impair the stability and permanency of the nation. Within these limitations, we hold it to be the duty of the government to inflict condign punishment on the rebel belligerents, and so weaken their hands that they can never again endanger the Union; and so reform their municipal institutions as to make them republican in spirit as well as in name.

We especially insist that the property of the chief rebels should be seized and appropriated to the payment of the National debt, caused by the unjust and wicked war which they instigated.

How can such punishments be inflicted and such forfeitures produced without doing violence to established principles?

Two positions have been suggested.

First – To treat those States as never having been out of the Union because the Constitution forbids secession, and therefore, a fact forbidden by law could not exist.

Second – To accept the position to which they placed themselves as severed from the Union; an independent government de facto, and an alien enemy to be dealt with according to the laws of war. . . .

. . . To say that they were States under the protection of that Constitution which they were rending, and within the Union which they were assaulting with bloody defeats, simply because they became belligerents through crime, is making theory overrule fact to an absurd degree. It will, I suppose, at least be conceded that the United States, if not obliged so to do, have a right to treat them as an alien enemy, now conquered, and subject to all the liabilities of a vanquished foe.

If we are also at liberty to treat them as never having been out of the Union, and that their declarations and acts were all void because they contravened the Constitution, and therefore they were never engaged in a public war, but were merely insurgents, let us inquire which position is best for the United States. If they have never been otherwise than States in the Union, and we desire to try certain of the leaders for treason, the Constitution requires that they should be indicted and tried "by an impartial jury of the State and district wherein the crime shall have been committed, which district shall have been previously ascertained by law."

. . . Select an impartial jury from Virginia, and it is obvious that no conviction could ever be had. Possibly a jury might be packed to convict, but that would not be an "impartial" jury. . . . The same difficulties would exist in attempting forfeitures, which can only follow conviction in States protected by the Constitution; and then it is said only for the life of the malefactor. Congress can pass no "bill of attainder."

Nor, under that theory, has Congress, much less the Executive, any power to interfere in remodeling those States upon reconstruction. . . . The sovereign power of the nation is lodged in Congress. Yet where is the warrant in the Constitution for such sovereign power, much less in the Executive, to intermeddle with the domestic institutions of a State, mold its laws, and regulate the elective franchise? It would be rank, dangerous and deplorable usurpation. In reconstruction, therefore, no reform can be effected in the Southern States if they have never left the Union. But reformation must be effected; the foundation of their institutions, both political, municipal and social, must be broken up and re-laid, or all our blood and treasure have been spent in vain. This can only be done by treating and holding them as a conquered people. Then all things which we can desire to do, follow with logical and legitimate authority. As conquered territory, Congress would have full power to legislate for them; for the territories are not under the Constitution, except so far as they express power to govern them is given to Congress. They would be held in a territorial condition until they are fit to form State constitutions, republican in fact, not in form only, and ask admission into the Union as new States. If Congress approves of their constitutions, and think they have done works meet for repentance, they would be admitted as new States. If their constitutions are not approved of, they would be sent back, until they have become wise enough so to purge their old laws as to eradicate every despotic and revolutionary principle—until they shall have learned to venerate the Declaration of Independence. I do not touch on the

question of negro suffrage. If in the Union, the States have long ago
regulated that, and for the Central Government to interfere with it
would be mischievous impertinence. If they are to be admitted as
new States they must form their own constitution; and no enabling
act could dictate its terms. Congress could prescribe the qualifications
of voters while a Territory, or when proceeding to call a convention to form a State government. That is the extent of the power of
Congress over the elective franchise, whether in a Territorial or State
condition. . . .

Upon the character of the belligerent, and the justice of the war, and
the manner of conducting it, depends our right to take the lives, liberty, and property of the belligerent. This war had its origin in treason
without one spark of justice. It was prosecuted before notice of it, by
robbing our forts and armories, and our navy-yards; by stealing our
money from the mints and depositories, and by surrendering our forts
and navies by perjurers who had sworn to support the Constitution.
In its progress our prisoners, by the authority of the government,
were slaughtered in cold blood. Ask Fort Pillow and Fort Wagner.[1]
Sixty thousand of our prisoners have been deliberately starved to
death because they would not enlist in the rebel armies. The graves at
Andersonville[2] have each an accusing tongue. The purpose and avowed
object of the enemy "to found an empire whose corner-stone should be
slavery,"[3] rendered its perpetuity or revival dangerous to human liberty.

Surely, these things are sufficient to justify the exercise of the
extreme rights of war—"to execute, to imprison, to confiscate." How

---

1. Confederate forces massacred black Union soldiers at Fort Pillow, April 1864. Stevens may be
referring to the Second Battle of Fort Wagner, July 1863. Following the battle Union dead were buried
by Confederates in a mass grave, but there was no massacre. https://teachingamericanhistory.org/library/
document/speech-on-reconstruction/#footnotes.

2. Andersonville was a Confederate prisoner of war camp near Andersonville, Georgia, notorious for its
terrible conditions. Nearly a third of the Union soldiers held there died. https://teachingamericanhistory.
org/library/document/speech-on-reconstruction/#footnotes.

3. Paraphrase of a remark in a speech by Thomas Hedges Genin (1796–1868), October 1865. Genin
was an Ohio Congressman. Genin was paraphrasing, as Stevens knew, the words of the Vice-President of
the Confederacy, Alexander Stephens (1812–1883), who in a speech delivered on March 21, 1861, said that
the Confederacy rests "its corner-stone . . . , upon the great truth that the negro is not equal to the white
man; that slavery – subordination to the superior race – is his natural and normal condition." The Georgia
legislature elected Stephens to the U.S. Senate in 1866, but the Senate refused to seat him. He served in the
U.S. House of Representatives from 1873 to 1882. https://teachingamericanhistory.org/library/document/
speech-on-reconstruction/#footnotes.

many captive enemies it would be proper to execute, as an example to nations, I leave others to judge. I am not fond of sanguinary punishments, but surely some victims must propitiate the manes[4] of our starved, murdered, slaughtered martyrs. A court-martial could do justice according to law.

But we propose to confiscate all the estate of every rebel belligerent whose estate was worth $10,000, or whose land exceeded two hundred acres in quantity. Policy, if not justice, would require that the poor, the ignorant, and the coerced should be forgiven. They followed the example and teachings of their wealthy and intelligent neighbors. . . .

What loyal man can object to this? Look around you, and everywhere behold your neighbors, some with an arm, some with a leg, some with an eye, carried away by rebel bullets. Others horribly mutilated in every form. And yet numerous others wearing the weeds which mark the death of those on whom they leaned for support. Contemplate these monuments of rebel perfidy, and of patriotic suffering, and then say if too much is asked for our valiant soldiers.

Look again, and see loyal men reduced to poverty by the confiscations by the Confederate States, and by the rebel States—see Union men robbed of their property, and their dwellings laid in ashes by rebel raiders, and say if too much is asked for them. But, above all, let us inquire whether imperative duty to the present generation and to posterity, does not command us to compel the wicked enemy to pay the expenses of this unjust war. In ordinary transactions, he who raises a false clamor, and prosecutes an unfounded suit, is adjudged to pay the costs on his defeat. We have seen that, by the law of nations, the vanquished in an unjust war must pay the expense. . . .

If "Restoration," as it is now properly christened, is to prevail over "Reconstruction," will some learned pundit of that school inform me in what condition slavery and the slave laws are? I assert that upon that theory [*restoration*] not a slave has been liberated, not a slave law has been abrogated, but on the "Restoration" the whole slave code is in legal force. Slavery was protected by our Constitution in every

---

4. Deceased, god-like spirits of ancestors. https://teachingamericanhistory.org/library/document/speech-on-reconstruction/#footnotes.

State in the Union where it existed. While they remained under that protection no power in the federal government could abolish slavery. If, however, the Confederate States were admitted to be what they claimed, an independent belligerent de facto, then the war broke all treaties, compacts, and ties between the parties, and slavery was left to its rights under the law of nations. These rights were none; for the law declares that "Man can hold no property in man." (Phillimore, page 316.)[5] Then the laws of war enabled us to declare every bondman free, so long as we held them in military possession. And the conqueror, through Congress, may declare them forever emancipated. But if the States are "States in the Union," then when war ceases they resume their positions with all their privileges untouched. There can be no "mutilated" restoration. That would be the work of Congress alone, and would be "Reconstruction." . . . is there some way to avoid hanging lines like this?

The whole fabric of Southern society must be changed, and never can it be done if this opportunity is lost. Without this, this government can never be, as it never has been, a true republic. Heretofore, it had more the features of aristocracy than of democracy. The Southern States have been despotisms, not governments of the people. It is impossible that any practical equality of rights can exist where a few thousand men monopolize the whole landed property. The larger the number of small proprietors the more safe and stable the government. As the landed interest must govern, the more it is subdivided and held by independent owners, the better. What would be the condition of the State of New York if it were not for her independent yeomanry? She would be overwhelmed and demoralized by the Jews, Milesians[6], and vagabonds of licentious cities. How can republican institutions, free schools, free churches, free social intercourse, exist in a mingled community of nabobs and serfs: of the owners of twenty-thousand-acre manors with lordly palaces, and the occupants of narrow huts

---

5. A reference perhaps to Robert Phillimore (1810–1885), an English jurist who wrote a commentary on international law. https://teachingamericanhistory.org/library/document/speech-on-reconstruction/#footnotes.

6. The Irish. https://teachingamericanhistory.org/library/document/speech-on-reconstruction/#footnotes.

inhabited by "low white trash?" If the South is ever to be made a safe republic, let her lands be cultivated by the toil of the owners, or the free labor of intelligent citizens. This must be done even though it drives her nobility into exile. If they go, all the better. It will be hard to persuade the owner of ten thousand acres of land, who drives a coach and four, that he is not degraded by sitting at the same table, or in the same pew, with the embrowned and hard-handed farmer who has himself cultivated his own thriving homestead of one hundred and fifty acres. This subdivision of the lands will yield ten bales of cotton to one that is made now, and he who produced it will own it and feel himself a man.

Let all who approve of these principles rally with us. Let all others go with Copperheads[7] and rebels. Those will be the opposing parties. Young men, this duty devolves on you. Would to God, if only for that, that I were still in the prime of life, that I might aid you to fight through this last and greatest battle of freedom!

(Palmer, Vol. 2, pp. 13–26)

---

7. Copperhead (after the poisonous snake of the same name) was a derisive term used by Republicans during the Civil War to describe Democratic politicians who wanted to negotiate a peace settlement with the South. https://teachingamericanhistory.org/library/document/speech-on-reconstruction/#footnotes.

Opening Remarks to the US Senate at the Impeachment Trial of Andrew Johnson, April 27, 1868

Hon. THADDEUS STEVENS, one of the Managers on behalf of the House of Representatives, addressed the Senate as follows:

Mr. Chief Justice, may it please the court, I trust to be able to be brief in my remarks, unless I should find myself less master of the subject which I propose to discuss than I hope. Experience has taught that nothing is so prolix as ignorance. I fear that I may prove thus ignorant, as I had not expected to take part in this debate until very lately. I shall discuss but a single article-the one that was finally adopted upon my earnest solicitation, and which, if proved, I considered then, and still consider, as quite sufficient for the ample conviction of the distinguished respondent and for his removal from office, which is the only legitimate object for which this impeachment could be instituted. During the very brief period which I shall occupy I declare to discuss the charges against the respondent in no mean spirit of malignity of vituperation, but to argue them in a manner worthy of the high tribunal before which I appear and of the exalted position of the accused. Whatever may be thought of his character of condition, he has been made respectable and his condition has been dignified by the action of his fellow citizens. Bailing accusation, therefore, would ill become this occasion, this tribunal, of a proper sense of the position of those who discuss this question on the one side or this other.

To see the chief servant of a trusting community arranged before the bar of public justice, charged with high delinquencies, is interesting. To behold the Chief Executive Magistrate of a powerful people charged with the betrayal of his trust, and arraigned for high crimes and misdemeanors, it always a most interesting spectacle. When the charges against such public servant accuse him of an attempt to betray the high trust confided in him and usurp the power of the whole people, that he may become their ruler, it is intensely interesting to millions of men, and should be discussed with a calm determination, which nothing can divert and nothing can reduce to mockery. Such is the condition of this great Republic, as looked upon by an astonished and wondering world. The offices of impeachment in England and America are very different from each other in the uses made of the for the punishment of offense and his will greatly err who undertakes to make out an analogy between them, either in the mode of trial or the final result. In England, the highest crimes may be tried before the high court of impeachment, and the severest punishments, even to imprisonment, fine, and death, may be inflicted. When our Constitution was from all these personal punishments were excluded from the judgment, and the defendant was to be dealt with just so far as the public safety required, and no further. Hence it was made to apply simply to the political offenses-to persons holding political positions, either my appointment or election by the people.

Thus, it is apparent that no crime containing malignant or indictable offenses high than misdemeanors was necessary either to be alleged or proved. If the respondent was shown to be abusing his official trust of the injury of the people for whom he was discharging public duties, and persevered in such abuse to the injury of his constituents, the true mode of dealing with him was to impeach him for the crimes or misdemeanors, (and only the latter is necessary,) and thus remove him from the office which he was abusing. Nor does it make a particle of difference whether such abuse arose from malignity, from unwarranted negligence, or from depravity, so repeated as to make his continuance in office injurious to the people and dangerous to the public welfare.

The punishment which the law, under our Constitution, authorizes to be inflicted, fully demonstrated this argument; that punishment upon conviction extends only to removal from office, and if the crime or misdemeanor charged be one of a deep and wicked dye the culprit is allowed to run at large, unless he should be pursued by a new prosecution in the ordinary courts. What does it matter, then, what the motive of the respondent might be in his repeated acts of malfeasance in office? Mere mistake in intention, is so persevered in after proper warning as to bring mischief upon the community, is quite sufficient to warrant the removal of the officer from the place where he is working mischief by his continuance in power.

The only question to be considered is: is the respondent violating the law. His perseverance in such a violation, although it shows a perverseness, is not absolutely necessary to his conviction. The great object is the removal from office and the arrest of the public injuries which he is inflicting upon those with whose interest he is entrusted.

The single charge which I had the honor to suggest I am expected to maintain. That duty is a light one, easily performed, and which, I apprehend, it will be found impossible for the respondent to answer or evade. When Andrew Johnson took upon himself the duties of his high office he swore to obey the Constitution and take care that the laws be faithfully executed. That, indeed, is and has always been the chief duty of the President of the United States. The duties of legislation and adjudicating the laws of his country fall in no way to his lot. To obey the commands of the sovereign power of the nation, and to see that others should obey them, was his whole duty-a duty which he could not escape, and any attempt to do so would be in direct violation of his official oath; in other words, a misprision of perjury.

I accuse him, in the name of the House of Representatives, of having perpetrated that foul offense against the laws and interests of his country.

Bibliography

_____, *Abraham Lincoln: Speeches and Writings 1859–1865*, The Library of America, 1989.

_____, *Pennsylvania Economy Factbook for 1992*, Harrisburg, Pennsylvania: 1992.

Angle, Paul M., ed., *The Lincoln Reader*, A Da Capo Paperback, 1990.

Blodgett, Harold W. and Sulley Bradley, eds. *Walt Whitman – Leaves of Grass*, New York, W.W. Norton and Company, Inc., 1965

Bloom, Allan, *Giants and Dwarfs*, New York: Simon and Schuster, 1990.

Bowen, Catherine Drinker, *Miracle at Philadelphia*, New York: Book of the Month Club, Inc., 1966.

Bradley, Sculley, ed., *The American Tradition in Literature*, Third Edition, New York: W.W. Norton and Company, 1967.

Brodie, Fawn M., *Thaddeus Stevens – Scourge of the South*, New York: W.W. Norton and Company, Inc., 1959

Brodie, Fawn, letter to Dr. Robert Fortenbaugh, July 26, 1956

Brooks, H.C.A., Address on 100th Anniversary of Peacham Academy, Aug. 11, 1897, courtesy of Adams County Historical Society

Byrd, Robert C., *The Senate, 1789–1989*, Washington, D.C.: U.S. Government Printing Office, 1988.

Cole, Donald B., and John J. McDonough, eds., *Witness to the Young Republic: A Yankee's Journal, 1828–1870*, Hanover: University Press of New England, 1989.

Couch, Ernie and Jill Couch, compilers, *Pennsylvania Trivia*, Nashville: Rutledge Hill Press, 1988.

Crabtree, Beth G. and James W. Patton, eds., *Journal of a Secesh Lady: The Diary of Catherine Ann Devereux Edmondston 1860–1866*, Raleigh: Division of Archives and History, 1979.

Crane, Stephen, *War is Kind*, New York: Barnes and Noble, 2007.

Current, Richard Nelson, *Old Thad Stevens, A Story of Ambition*, Madison: The University of Wisconsin Press, 1942.

Dickens, Charles, *American Notes*, Gloucester, Massachusetts: Peter Smith Publishing, 1968.

Eisenhower, Dwight D., *At Ease: Stories I Tell to Friends*, New York: Doubleday and Company, Inc., 1967.

Emerson, Edward W., *Life and Letters of Charles Russell Lowell*, Port Washington, New York: Kennikat Press, 1971.

Foner, Eric, and Olivia Mahoney, *A House Divided – America in the Age of Lincoln*, New York: Chicago Historical Society in association with W.W. Norton and Company, 1990

Foner, Eric, *Free Soil, Free Labor, Free Men: The Ideology of the Republican Party Before the Civil War*, New York: Oxford University Press, 1970

Friedman, Milton and Rose, *Free to Choose*. New York: Harcourt Brace Jovanovich, 1980.

Gallagher, Gary W., ed., *Fighting for the Confederacy: The Personal Recollections of General Edward Porter Alexander*, Chapel Hill: The University of North Carolina Press, n.d.

Garreau, Joel, *The Nine Nations of North America*, New York: Avon Books, 1981.

Haber, Barbara Angle, *Pennsylvania*, New York: Gallery Books – A Division of W. H. Smith Publishers, Inc., 1991.

Hensel, William Uhler, *Thaddeus Stevens as a Country Lawyer*, Harrisburg: State Library of Pennsylvania, n.d.

Hoch, Bradley R., *Thaddeus Stevens in Gettysburg: The Making of an Abolitionist*, Adams County Historical Society and Bradley R. Hoch, 2005.

Johnston, William B., project director, *Workforce 2000: Work and Workers for the Twenty-First Century*, Indianapolis: Hudson Institute, 1987.

Katz, Joseph, ed., *The Portable Stephen Crane*, New York: The Viking Press, 1969.

Kennedy, John F., *Profiles in Courage*, Memorial Edition, New York: Harper and Row, 1964

Klein, Philip S. and Ari Hoogenboom, *A History of Pennsylvania*, University Park, Pennsylvania: The Pennsylvania State University Press, 1980.

Korngold, Ralph, *Thaddeus Stevens: A Being Darkly Wise and Rudely Great*, New York: Harcourt Brace and Company, 1955.

Kozol, Jonathan, *Savage Inequalities Children in America's Schools*, New York: Crown Publishers, Inc., 1991.

Levine, Louis, project director, *The Potential for Human Resources and Economic Growth in a Declining Local Community: A Socio-Economic Study of Johnstown, Pennsylvania*, University Park, Pennsylvania, The Institute for Research on Human Resources at the Pennsylvania State University,1969.

McCall, Samuel W., *Thaddeus Stevens*, New York: Houghton, Mifflin and Company, 1899.

McPherson, James M., *The Negro's Civil War: How the American Negros Felt and Acted During the War for the Union*, Chicago: University of Illinois Press, n.d.

Moore, Daniel, ed., *Warrior Wisdom*, Philadelphia: Running Press,1993.

Morrison, Samuel Eliot, *The Oxford History of the American People, V. 2*, New York: Penguin Books, 1972

Myers, Robert Manson, ed., *The Children of Pride: A True Story of Georgia and the Civil War*, New Haven: Yale University Press, 1972.

Naisbitt, John, *Megatrends: Ten New Directions Transforming Our Lives*, New York: Warner Books, 1982.

O'Connor, John C. and Yeager, Ralph M.(collection), *Pennsylvania Prints*, University Park, Pennsylvania: The Pennsylvania State University Museum of Art, 1980.

Osborne, David, and Ted Gaebler, *Reinventing Government: How the Entrepreneurial Spirit is Transforming the Public Sector*, New York: Addison Wesley Publishing Company, Inc., 1992.

Palmer, Beverly Wilson and Holly Byers Ochoa, Editor and Associate Editor, *The Selected Papers of Thaddeus Stevens*, University of Pittsburgh Press, 1997.

Reeves, Richard, *American Journey*, New York: Simon and Schuster, 1982.

Roberts, Michael, ed., (revised by Peter Porter), *The Faber Book of Modern Verse*, Boston: Faber and Faber, 1982 (4th ed.)

Singmaster, Elsie, *I Speak for Thaddeus Stevens*

Slater, Michael, ed., *Dickens on America and the Americans*, Austin: University of Texas Press, 1978.

Smith, George Winston and Charles Judah, *Life in the North During the Civil War: A Source History*, The University of New Mexico Press, n.d.

Solomon, Eric, ed., *The Faded Banners – A Treasury of Nineteenth Century Civil War Fiction*, New York: Promontory Press, 1992.

Stampp, Kenneth M., *The Imperiled Union: Essays on the Background of the Civil War*, New York: Oxford University Press, 1980.

Strauss, William and Neil Howe, *Generations: The History of America's Future, 1584–2069*, New York: Quill, 1991

Updike, John, *Hugging the Shore: Essays and Criticism*, New York: Alfred A. Knopf, 1983.

Van Den Heuvel, Cor, ed., *The Haiku Anthology*, New York: Touchstone (Simon and Schuster), 1986.

Warch, Richard and Jonathan Fanton, eds., *John Brown*, Englewood Cliffs, N.J., Prentice-Hall, Inc., 1973.

Ward, Geoffrey C., Ken Burns and Richard Burns, *The Civil War*, New York: Penguin Random House, 1994

Weigley, Russell F., editor, *Philadelphia: A 300 Year History*, New York: W.W. Norton and Company, 1982.

Wendel, Thomas Harold, *The Life and Writings of Sir William Keith, Lieutenant Governor of Pennsylvania and the Three Lower Counties, 1717–1726*, Ann Arbor: University Microfilms, Inc.,1964.

Whittier, John Greenleaf, *The Poetical Works of John Greenleaf Whittier, Volume IV*, New York: Houghton Mifflin Company, 1892.

Wills, Garry, *Lincoln at Gettysburg: The Words that Remade America*, New York: Simon and Schuster, 1992.

Woodburn, James Albert, *The Life of Thaddeus Stevens*, New York: Bobbs-Merrill Company, 1940.

Woodley, Thomas Frederick, *Thaddeus Stevens*, Harrisburg: The Telegraph Press, 1934.

Woodley, Thomas Frederick, *The Great Leveler – The Life of Thaddeus Stevens*, New York: Stackpole Sons, 1937.

Woodward, C. Vann, ed., *Mary Chestnut's Civil War*, New Haven: Yale University Press,1981.

Yanak, Ted and Pam Cornelison, *The Great American History Fact-Finder*, New York: Houghton Mifflin Company, 1993.

Index

[A]
Anti-Masons, 62, 66, 67, 70, 132

[B]
Beauregard, Pierre, 124
Beecher, Henry Ward, 128
Beers, Paul, 2
Berlucchy, C. N., 43
Bigelow, Hosea, 114
Black, Jeremiah, 35
Blair, Montgomery, 144, 145, 146
Blanchard, Jonathan, 29, 30, 31, 36, 37, 38, 39, 40, 41, 47, 61, 76
Bowles, Samuel, 14
Brodie, Fawn, vi, 5, 77
Brooks, H. C. A., 18
Brooks, Preston, 123
Brown, John, 86, 87, 88, 89, 90, 91, 110, 128
Bruce, Norman, 23, 26, 27
Buchanan, James, 1, 3, 103, 106, 110, 111, 112, 113, 143
Burrowes, Thomas, 65, 71, 72, 73
Butler, Benjamin, 147
Butler, Charity, 23, 24, 26, 43

[C]
Calhoun, John C., 106, 118, 119
Cameron, Simon, 79, 106, 145, 146
Cass, Lewis, 119
Cassatt, Jacob, 73
Chase, Salmon, 79, 119
Chester, Morris T., 125
Christiana Riots, 81, 123
Clay Compromise, 114, 119
Clay, Henry, 61, 63, 114, 119, 120
Cobb, Howell, 131
Coleman, Ann, 1, 110

Cooper, James, 65
Crane, Stephen, 110
Cunningham, T. S., 71, 72, 73
Current, Richard Nelson, v, 4, 77
Curtin, Andrew, 106, 145

[D]
Dangerfield, John, 88
Davis, Jefferson, 105, 119, 127, 128, 130
Dennison, William, 146
DePerigord, Talleyrand, 13, 15
DeTocqueville, Alexis, 91, 107
Dinah, 5, 6, 24, 25, 27, 28, 29, 32, 35, 36, 38, 43, 44, 45, 47, 48, 49, 56, 59, 60
Dobbins, James, 24, 46
Douglas, Stephen, 106, 119
Drake, George, 14
Dred Scott Decision, 124

[E]
Edmonston, Catherine, 126
Edwards, Jonathan, 38
Elmaker, Amos, 65, 111
Emerson, Ralph W., 7, 92, 106, 114
Euripides, 16
Everett, Edward, 135, 136

[F]
Fenn, Theophilus, 65
Fillmore, Millard, 118
Fletcher, David, 33, 34, 35
Ford, Gerald, 1
Forten, James, 116
Fortenbaugh, Robert, 5
Freemasonry, 61, 65
Fremont, John C., 91, 146
French, Benjamin Brown, 112
Fugitive Slave Law, 104, 120, 121, 122

[G]
Galloway, Samuel, 79
Garcia-Marquez, Gabriel, 7
Garrison, William Lloyd, 91, 93, 106, 112, 114
Gavin, John, 45
Gettys, James, 21
Gettysburg Centinel, 45
Gettysburg Compiler, 44
Giddings, Joshua, 119
Gorsuch, Dickinson, 122
Gorsuch, Edward, 122, 123
Greeley, Horace, 106, 112, 144

[H]
Hamlin, Hannibal, 119, 159
Harper's Ferry, 85
Hawthorne, Nathaniel, 93, 114
Hersh, George, 28, 43, 44
Hoch, Bradley, vi, 78
Hopkins, Henry, 71, 73

[J]
Jackson, Andrew, 61, 63, 111
Jay, John, 79
Johnson, Andrew, 19, 92, 113, 119, 157, 158, 159, 160, 163, 165
Jung, Carl, 7

[K]
Kennedy, John F., 120, 165
Korngold, Ralph, 77

[L]
Lawrence, D.H., 107, 170
Lee, Robert E., 88, 91, 93, 136, 138, 139, 140
LeFever, Jacob, 34, 55, 56, 57, 62
Lincoln, Abraham, 4, 33, 80, 87, 88, 92, 103, 104, 105, 106, 107, 110, 112, 117, 125, 127, 135, 136, 137, 139, 142, 143, 153, 154, 156, 159
Lincoln, Willie, 137

Lippman, Walter, 107
Longfellow, Henry Wadsworth, 91, 114
Lovejoy, Owen, 112, 124
Lowell, James Russell, 114

[M]
Mann, Horace, 119
Mattock, John, 12, 17, 38
McCahen, John J., 71, 72
McFarlane, John, 46
McLintock, John, 79
McPherson, Emma, 45
McPherson, William, 34
Mellins, W. B., 77
Meredith, William, 70, 116
Missouri Compromise, 22, 114
Moore, Daniel, 109
Morgan, William, 60, 61, 66
Mott, James, 116
Mott, Lucretia, 116
Muhlenberg, Henry, 66, 112

[O]
O'Neill, Keziah, 34, 35, 48

[P]
Palmer, Beverly, vi
Panic of 1837, 69
Parker, William, 122
Penrose, Charles B., 72, 73
Philadelphia, 67, 68, 71, 72
Phillips, Wendell, 90
Pope, Alexander, 21, 28
Porter, David, 70, 112

[R]
Randolph, John, 119
Reconstruction, 157
Reed, Thurlow, 61
Reeves, Robert, 107
Ritner, Joseph, 66, 69, 70, 73
Ross, Edmund, 166, 167, 168, 169

[S]
Schlesinger, Arthur, 113
Sergeant, John, 79, 116
Seventh of March Speech, 120
Seward, William, 62, 79, 119, 135
Shaw, George Bernard, 87
Singmaster, Elsie, 4, 35, 77
Smith, Lydia Hamilton, 3, 35, 75, 78, 107, 133, 154, 155, 169
Stanton, Edwin, 161, 162
Stevens, Abner, 15
Stevens, Alexander, 106, 119
Stevens, Allanson, 15, 133, 154
Stevens, Joshua, 14, 15
Stevens, Sarah, 13, 16, 107
Stevens, Thaddeus, Jr., 60, 133
Still, William, 116, 123
Strauss, William, 90, 93
Stuart, J. E. B., 88, 89
Sumner, Charles, 112, 114, 123, 159

[T]
Taylor, Zachary, 80, 118
Thirteenth Amendment, 153

Thompson, William, 60
Toombs, Robert, 119, 128

[U]
Updike, John, 1, 3

[V]
Van Buren, Martin, 112

[W]
Wade, Ben, 112, 101, 162
Webster, Daniel, 106, 119, 120, 121
Welles, Gideon, 156
Wheelock, Edwin M., 89
Whig Party, 63, 70, 71, 79, 80
Whitman, Walt, 92, 115
Whittier, John Greenleaf, 106, 108, 115, 122, 142
Wilmot Proviso, 118
Wirt, William, 62
Wolf, George, 63, 64, 65, 66, 112
Woodley, Thomas, vi
Woodward, George, 22
Wordsworth, William, 25, 28, 54

About the Author

Mark is "of counsel" to the McNees Winter Group in Harrisburg. From 1987 through 1995, Singel was Lieutenant Governor and, for a period of time, Acting Governor of the Commonwealth. The only person in Pennsylvania history to serve an extended period as Acting Governor, Singel received high marks for his stewardship. He led the state by enacting the first modern workers' compensation reform package, refinanced the state's park system through the "Key 93" program, and helped launch the high-tech era with landmark telecommunications legislation. He was also instrumental in reducing state and local taxes, the implementation of a statewide 911 emergency phone system, and the creation of thousands of new jobs in recycling and environmental technologies. He was the original author of the state's mortgage assistance bill that has saved 35,000 Pennsylvania homes.

Prior to his terms as Lieutenant Governor, Singel served six years in the Pennsylvania State Senate and was chief of staff to two members of the U.S. Congress.

Singel ran for U.S. Senate in 1992 and for Governor in 1994. He served as Chairman of the Pennsylvania Democratic Party from 1995–1998 and was the President of Pennsylvania's Electoral College in January 1997.

Upon leaving public service, he founded Singel Associates and later established The Winter Group which developed into one of the most effective and prestigious government relations firms in the state. The Winter Group is now part of the McNees Wallace family of legal and governmental services.

Singel served as chairman of Governor Ed Rendell's Transition Executive Committee and maintains strong personal and political ties with leaders at all levels today. He is a known Harrisburg "insider" with a reputation for getting results.

A magna cum laude graduate of Penn State, Singel has served on the Boards of Penn State and St. Francis Universities. He holds several honorary doctorate degrees. He is the author of a book about his service as Acting Governor entitled *A Year of Change and Consequences* and is completing work on several new writing projects. Singel is a regular commentator on local and statewide political broadcast programs. He is a sought-after speaker at both political and academic events and is active in numerous community and philanthropic activities. He currently serves as the Vice Chair, Board of Directors, Harrisburg University of Science and Technology.

Singel has been married to Jacqueline for over 45 years and has three children and five grandchildren.

www.ingramcontent.com/pod-product-compliance
Lightning Source LLC
Chambersburg PA
CBHW021400090426
42742CB00009B/931